To Dave Newell

From

James Hewitt

CW01648926

To Wyn

to my family and relatives
without whom this book could not have been published

Acknowledgments

Thanks are due to
Nicola Dolderson of H_2O
and also to
Tony Condor, Paul Sillitoe, Diana Sumner and Roy Jamieson of the Waterways Trust
To Annete Price for proofreading the text

Where oaken gates resist the stream
Where pent up water reigns supreme
Where heavy laden barge is seen
There you will find a navigation

James Hewitt

ADVENTURES

of

THE NIPPY

by

James Hewitt

ISBN
0 9543197 0 2

All design and computer work
by
h2o
ndolderson@home2office.demon.co.uk
01257 273747

Printed
by
T Snape & Company Limited, Boltons Court, Preston, Lancashire PR1 3TY

CONTENTS

ILLUSTRATIONS

All illustrations and maps kindly produced by Edward Paget-Tomlinson

MAPS

ILLUSTRATIONS

PHOTOGRAPHS

All photographs belong to the author except where otherwise stated

PHOTOGRAPHS

(continued)

INTRODUCTION

We are living in a second canal age. All over the country there is work going forward to open again a considerable mileage of waterways, which many enthusiasts had not expected to be revived.

One canal, the Huddersfield Narrow, is taken up the Pennines by a ladder of locks, plunging through Standege the longest canal tunnel in the country. A new navigation nearly four miles in length is being constructed not far from where I live, connecting the Lancaster with that intricate network of waterways built so many years ago. They were originally intended for commercial use but now are an outlet for those wishing to explore the countryside, nowadays with official approval.

It has not always been the case. Many canals had gone into railway hands to be nationalised with them in 1948. They had been declining for years owing to a lack of proper investment. The British Transport Commission sought to close a great mileage in the Transport Bill of 1955 and there was talk in official circles of 'cutting out the dead wood'. Luckily, it did not happen for there were enthusiasts around even then who put up a spirited resistance, yet the threat continued for a number of years like a dark cloud hanging over the system. The answer lay in using the waterways as much as possible, especially those most under threat, and confrontation was inevitable.

The book mostly talks about the exploits of NIPPY, a homemade motor cruiser built by my father which travelled the waterways at that time. We took her through a canal very much against the wishes of British Waterways who threatened us with legal action. This canal, the Ashton, was closed for a while when we joined with others in a reopening campaign which eventually was successful.

In later years I joined British Waterways 'on the bank' in order to gain much valuable experience which included steering the famous PRESIDENT, formerly driven by steam and since restored to her original glory. Other experiences included dealing with a full-scale breach in addition to the daily work of running a canal, giving information never published before.

This book is not really about NIPPY or any of her crew. It is about the waterways of England upon which she sailed, and if anyone in reading it learns a little of those waterways and what they are all about then its purpose will have been served.

James Hewitt

March 2002

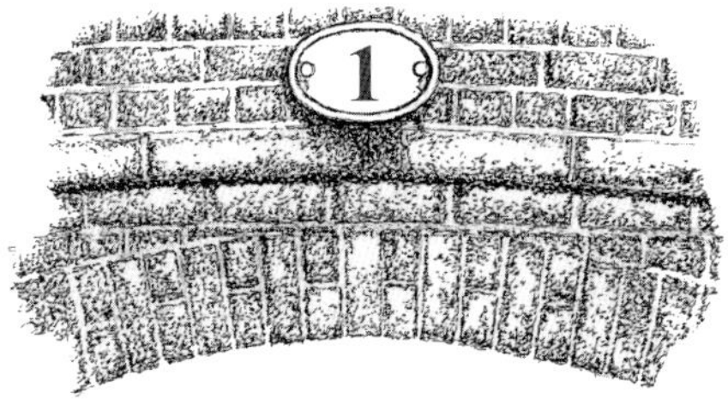

Early Days

It all began when we moved home. Formerly this had been a quiet and undistinguished suburb just outside Manchester, but in 1946, when I was around six or seven we moved, my father and mother and I, to the more industrial scene of Clayton on the eastern side of that city.

Gone were the endless rows of neat suburbia. Instead, our windows looked out upon warehouses and factories busy on all sides, for this part of Manchester was very active then with chemical and engineering works. Our home actually belonged to the largest manufacturer in the area where my father lived as part of his job. Only one area still belonged to nature. A defiant swathe of reed-fringed water provided a home for waterhens and other wildlife. This vital strip of nature passed close by our home. It was a canal.

The canal was crossed by a main road bridge with a heavy door set into the parapet on each side of the bridge and sometimes a man would be seen roughly dressed, carrying a heavy coil of rope over his shoulder, crossing from one side to the other. I soon learned the reason for this and would hover expectantly around the end of the bridge. Firstly came the slow click clack of iron-shod clogs, which some working folk still wore at that time. This heralded the arrival of a laden craft with a man laid on some sacking, propelling her along with his feet against the low, level span of the bridge. The bridge was relatively long with no towpath through it. This was known as legging, and must have been a common sight during the days of horse drawn craft. Many canal tunnels have no towing path, so the horse would be taken over the hill whilst the remaining crew legged the boat through in a practice that only died out when powered craft came along. Their method was to lay one each side of the bows on boards or 'wings' which enabled them to reach the tunnel sides with their feet.

I marvelled at the length of the seventy-foot craft as she emerged through the bridge. She was a dayboat, that is to say she was without living accommodation, being purely for the carriage of cargo. The towline would be connected again and off they would go one bowhauling and the other shafting the boat along, keeping her in the centre with some difficulty, for this was only a narrow branch canal off the main line. And so they would recede into the distance with their load of acid, sulphuric I believe, though one hardly supposed at so deadly a load gliding between the reedy banks.

As I grew older I discovered more about the little arm of canal which actually was not so small, being about half or three quarters of a mile long. It was called the Clayton or Schofields arm after the firm owning the acid boat and made a junction with the Ashton Canal between locks seven and eight.

We were all hooked on the inland waterways by that time and decided to try a holiday on the Norfolk broads, going several times, the first being restricted as it coincided with the final week of petrol rationing. The broads were much quieter then of course, which I can only describe as a blessing since we ran the usual gamut of mistakes and misadventures almost obligatory for the novice. One tends to look back on these with a smile although they are not so humorous at the time.

One morning, leaving the town of Norwich, we came across the coaster ZUYPE coming the other way through a narrows where a lift bridge spanned the river. We eased the engine down on our hire cruiser and went into reverse, and the engine cut out! Carried forward by our momentum and by the water sluicing past the ship, we were drawn into the gap between her and the shore, ricocheting from one to the other. We heard the slow, pumping note of her engine before spotting another hazard – cooling water was jetting out from her side and advancing along our deck to saturate us all. We had to take it as we stood since nobody fancied going below. The captain stood at the end of her bridge bawling down at us with a megaphone, whereby my father replied in equal fashion needing no megaphone to amplify his remarks. One final thump and we were through with the captains of both vessels still exchanging strident comment across the widening gap.

We managed to start our engine and limped into the yacht moorings at Thorpe, from where we contacted the boatyard in Wroxham. Our message that we had collided with a ship must have sent them into something akin to panic for a little van buzzed into the yard soon afterwards and two of their men got out and shot over to the boat. We had been lucky. The only damage taken had been a buckled porthole rim, a few scratches none of them deep, plus a leaking seacock, which they soon tightened. The faulty engine was examined and adjusted. We continued on our way but gave shipping a very wide berth after that.

About this time I discovered the peaceful tranquillity of simply letting the anchor go and fetching up in some broad or other, Wroxham perhaps, then exploring the area in the dinghy whilst the hire cruiser meandered around its cable. My mother liked the fact that she had a different view every time she looked out of the window as the soft summer breeze swung us round this way and that. Sometimes a school friend would also come along and we loved to wander around the boat building yards where wood was still king and there was always a wonderful scent of mahogany and oak and of freshly applied varnish. Nobody could argue about the practical superiority of fibreglass as a boat building material and nowadays I have a seagoing craft with the hull of fibreglass, and a very suitable construction it really is with never a leak through some faulty seam. Yet there is something satisfying about owning a craft well made in wood, and of course everything deteriorates in time. Wood goes rotten, steel rusts, whilst fibreglass is prone to osmosis.

Going hire cruising once a year is all very well but I pined for having a boat of my own and I think that my father fancied the idea of building one, being a practical man who liked to solve problems of a practical nature. He bought an American book which contained details of several small craft suitable for the amateur to build and finally settled on one, a six foot rowing and sailing dinghy, and decided that it would be suitable for me since I was then around ten years old. We then commenced to build it. I could hardly wait to go sailing and its construction seemed to take an age. He was in charge of the fire brigade at a dyestuffs and chemicals manufacturer, and the boat was built in the corner of the fire station. There we would work sometimes late into the night with me standing holding a torch to give additional light.

He was regarded as being something of a hero by many of his contemporaries, since the works at that time was a fairly dangerous place with fires and explosions, of which there were many incidents by day and night. Often the telephone would ring in the small hours and he would be up in an instant, answering it briefly then charging off into the night to deal with some problem reported by the works police. Sometimes they would panic and send for the Manchester fire brigade instead but he was always vexed about that. They did more damage than the fire to valuable dyestuffs with their practice of spraying everything in sight with gallons of water. "Never panic at the sight of a fire, but deal with it or send for me", he would urge the police and the workforce in general. He himself seemed quite fearless and I have seen him enter a smoke filled building with everyone else running out.

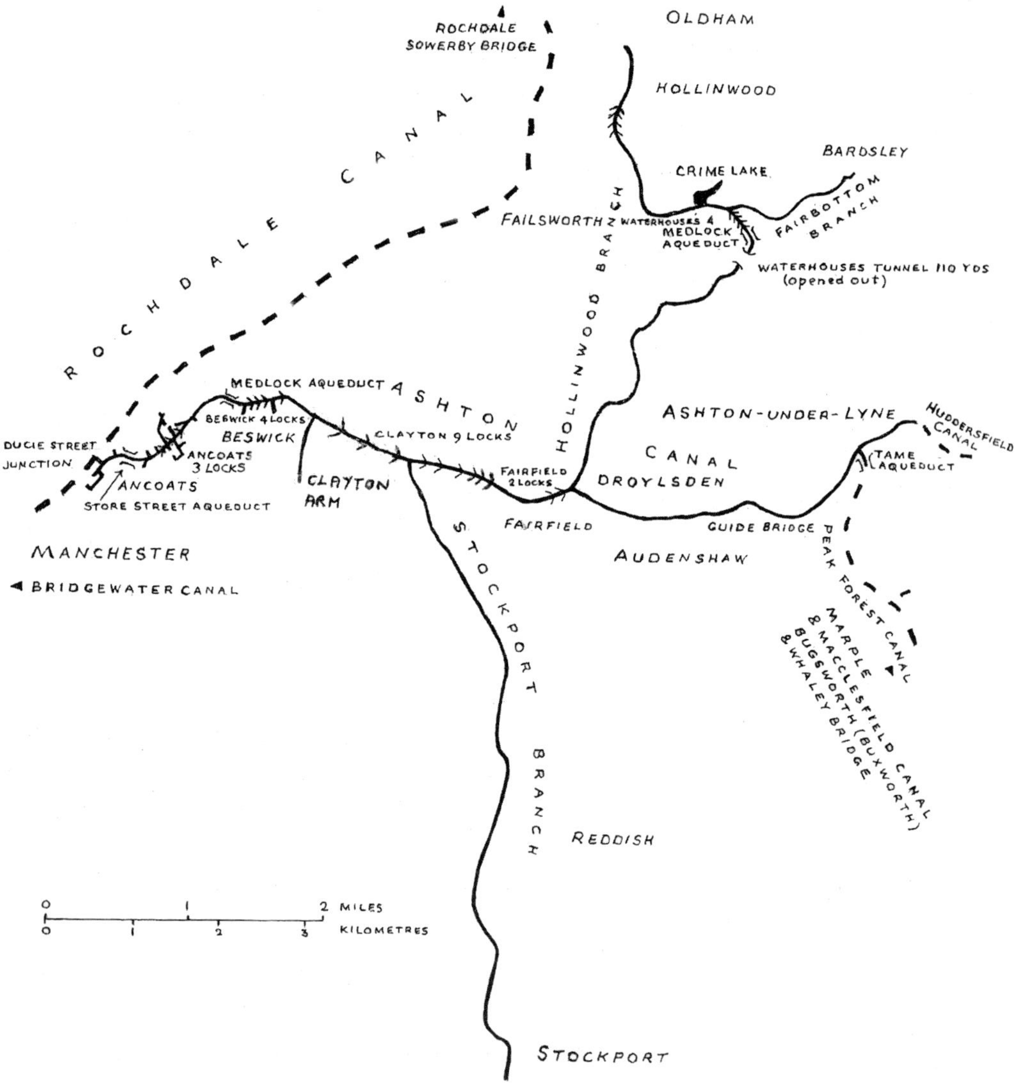

Ashton Canal and Branches
(illustrated by Edward Paget-Tomlinson)

One day they called him to the scene where a man had gone berserk and was occupying a warehouse in the works, firing indiscriminately with a revolver. My father counted the shots until he knew the gun was empty, then stepped out briskly before it could be reloaded. "Right Tom Mix, give us that," he said, holding out his hand. The man stared for a moment then meekly handed it over.

Eventually my little boat was completed and duly launched with ceremony and so began my exploration of the canal system which has continued with a number of craft over forty years and more. The boat proved to be a hit with my schoolmates as we enjoyed many boating and fishing expeditions, often overloaded, with sometimes a watery conclusion, in addition to our usual activities during those summer months when the world seemed a much gentler place and children could wander without fear of being attacked. There was hardly a need to warn us not to accept sweets from strangers or if anything it was the other way round. "Go an buy yer bloody own" we would be told after the usual entreaty but we always came back to the canal. Mostly we sailed up and down the arm but sometimes would chance a trip along the main line itself which was of course much wider and deeper. Eventually we would be spotted by Walter Wood the lock keeper at Mill Street and his shouted instructions sent us scuttling back to the safety of the privately owned little arm since we had no licence for the Ashton, and besides Walter was known to be on a short fuse at times.

Although the acid traffic had been stopped for several years the day boats that had carried it still remained, being sunk next to the premises of Schofields. One day a group of men appeared with buckets and bailed one out. We were amazed to see her gradually come up as they toiled away and volunteered our services. "Grab a bucket then" one said, so we set to with a will. They were a rough looking lot and heaven knows what they intended to do with her, but eventually by evening time the boat was dry and riding to its moorings, afloat once more. They left her there for a week or so, warning us not to play on her but of course we did and nearly put their plans asunder. On walking about the hold, one of us stood on a bolt so corroded it dropped straight out through the bottom and there was an immediate spout of water. We rushed around in search of something to plug it with, telling the men when they returned. They were somewhat disgruntled at first to discover our trespass but glad we had highlighted what could for them be a serious problem. If we had found one corroded bolt, there would be others.

Their first intention was to sail her to Stretford Dry Dock on the Bridgewater Canal where they said Schofield's boats had always been repaired, and after buying her for sixty pounds they set off closely followed by us in our little craft. All went well until we gained the lock at Mill Street, the gates freshly painted in their livery of brown and white and there stood Walter in wait for us. "Now then gents, where are you going with that boat?" Then seeing us paddling around in the background he erupted in fury. "I've told you before to shift that bloody boat," he bawled as we prepared for a hasty retreat. "They've no licence you see," he explained to them. "Well neither have we," they told him, looking at one another and it turned out that nobody was going anywhere. Their boat was tied up on the offside above Mill Street Lock where she sank and remained for many years.

But the germ of an idea had settled upon us which would not go away, for there remained yet another suitable sunken boat. We laid our plans and awaited an opportunity.

Came the Whitsuntide and Schofields closed for the holidays whereupon an observer would have seen several lads boarding a sunken narrow boat and setting to with buckets, basins and anything else available. How long does it take a group of lads to bail out such a boat? The answer is about a day and a half for she was settled more deeply than the other. Still toiling away we took stock of our prize, noting the simple construction and shape and the name NORA carved indelibly into her bow. Of course she was just a fall about old boat by that time with many rotting timbers, but we bailed her out completely and she leaked not a drop. We were delighted with her. Using poles and assorted lengths of wood we propelled our new acquisition along at a fair speed and hid her under Ashton New Road Bridge, which happened to be wide enough to conceal her length whilst the lack of towpath gave an added sense of security. Here we dropped anchor using stones and lumps of concrete tied to old rope. Surveying our handiwork as we rowed away, we felt very pleased indeed with ourselves and our achievement.

We discussed wider journeys along the Ashton itself at great length, which fortunately never came to anything since poor Walter would surely have suffered a heart attack, however, not everyone shared in our euphoria.

The manager of Schofields returned to the works at the end of holidays and could not help noticing that a boat sunken for years outside his office had now disappeared. He was not long in settling upon the most likely culprits. We were told that he sought an early interview with us by one of his workmen, grinning from ear to ear. So we decided to make ourselves scarce but he cornered us. "Where's my boat," he yelled and we had the feeling that he was vexed but eventually he calmed down. "Look lads," he said, "that boat carried acid for years and it could still be impregnated into the timbers for all I know. Tell you what," he continued, "give me five pounds for her and that will be the end of my responsibility." Regretfully, we did not have five pounds, even between the lot of us, so the manager laid plans of his own. His men were instructed to make a raft constructed of planks and drums, and with many a roll and wobble they finally boarded the narrow boat still hidden under the bridge. The craft was drawn out, taken to the end of the arm and permanently sunk, drifting across the canal as she went down which thus broke her back.

Naturally, we all felt pretty depressed at this. From our point of view we had done something positive whilst the manager had responded with a destructive act, although in retrospect he could hardly have done anything else since he was still responsible for the boat. My parents were quick to notice the effect this had on me and I think that it provided a trigger for us to obtain a boat large enough to explore the inland waterways in which we were all interested. A book had just been published called 'The Canals of England', by Eric de Mare, which gave an enticing glimpse of the English canal system as seen through the eyes of an architect and writer, and with many excellent photos it remains one of the best ever written on the subject.

Nowadays, the intending boat-owner is faced with a bewildering array of boatyards all anxious to provide him or her with a craft, from a basic hull to the finished article including the engine of their choice. Similarly the second hand market has a wide range available dependent only on the enthusiast's taste and depth of pocket. Things were different in the early fifties. The industry of building narrow boats for pleasure had not begun. There were far fewer pleasure boats around, and of those that did exist, the majority had been converted from something else, perhaps a full or part length former working narrow boat, usually made of wood and obtained cheaply from one of the carriers operating then, Horsfields perhaps on the Bridgewater or Thomas Claytons in the black country. Then there were the ships' lifeboats, which could make an attractive conversion in the right hands. The Bridgewater Canal enthusiasts were lucky in that they did not have to seek a lifeboat restricted to a seven-foot beam, which presented a problem to those wishing to use the narrow canal system. One owner that I knew, having bought a steel lifeboat, moved it to his back garden and then discovered that she was slightly too wide in the beam. Undeterred by this he bought a fourteen-pound hammer and early one Sunday morning began to reduce the offending dimension to the interest of his neighbours!

Another school of thought lent towards the purchase of an ex-Army bridging pontoon, for once again these were very cheap and owing to their shape not difficult to convert. One drawback to this type of conversion was that with their shallow draught and high boxy cabin, they were able to move forwards or sideways with equal facility in the slightest wind.

Life for the pleasure cruising enthusiast was much different then and few people understood what it was really all about. The press regarded these intrepid navigators as being little better than a bunch of eccentrics, which in a number of cases was not far off the mark. What they all possessed in fullest measure was an enthusiasm that enabled them to fit out a boat and to range all over the canal system with scant information available on anything, each perhaps in one sense a pioneer in his own right. And my parents had decided to join this little band.

Considering the options for conversion one by one, my father eventually decided that he would build a motor cruiser of his own after finding a good design and it was here that he met with his first problem, for nobody really designed a craft intended for the inland waterways or not as far as he knew, so it had to be a compromise.

He finally settled upon a stretched version of the Rutland Cruiser by Harold Dawes, and in using the word stretched I should perhaps add that even in this form she only measured eighteen feet eight inches in length. Intended as a river and estuary cruiser for fishermen, she would have been ideal for the purpose, but as a family cruiser intended to stay aboard for lengthy periods, she was to prove rather small, although we only came to this conclusion by degrees. She seemed quite roomy enough when looking at the plans, which we pored over by the hour and which were shown to a friend of his who was co-director of a joinery works in Manchester, noted for its excellent quality of timber and workmanship.

Invited to inspect their works, we were first taken to the mill, where accompanied by a great cacophony of sound we found a variety of machines at work. To one side a four cutter was producing tongue and groove boards with labourers carefully stacking the resultant whippy planks for storage and distribution. Entering gratefully the quiet kiln area, there were planks seasoning in the warm atmosphere produced by burning the waste products of the mill. Going onwards and into the yard itself, great logs were awaiting their turn, timber of all descriptions from all parts of the world. Certainly there was no lack of material from which to make a selection and my father went over the matter very carefully with the director, assisted by his foreman, and eventually made his choice. The boat was to be built in a warehouse of the works, chosen because it was cleaner than most and had been partly let off to a firm that made boxes and casks. We cleared a space and impatiently waited for the timber to arrive and were not disappointed when it did.

A beautifully figured piece of oak already shaped to size had been provided for the stempost with fore apron and cutwater in the same material. The hog, keel, chines and fillets were all of greenheart, very heavy without any traces of knot. Dark mahogany for the frames, stringers, butt straps and knees, with the deck beams also in mahogany but made up in glued laminate form. A stack of marine plywood completed the initial order and I wondered how on earth we were ever going to turn it into a boat. I was to find out the hard way!

Firstly, the eight frames were set out and each assembled in the front bedroom using brass screws and aerolite glue, which we found to be very strong. All of this was endured by my mother, whom I have to say put up with a great deal with very little complaint. The next step was to carry them to the proposed building site about half a mile away, one by one. I should at this point say to any potential boat builder that the boat needs to be constructed as near as possible to the home, since the journey from home to boatyard has often to be made and can be a chore at times. I once knew somebody who fitted out quite a small craft and took years to finish it, not because he was a slow worker, but due instead to the boat being fifty miles or more from his home. The best arrangement is where she is within easy walking distance and the builder can be home from work, have his tea and then nip out to do an hour or two in the evening. Returning to the job in hand, we first of all laid eight railway sleepers on the concrete floor and screwed wooden blocks to both ends of each. The frames were then fastened to these, upside down with the length of each frame being exact and taken off the full size offset plans for the boat. Each one had a datum line marked on it, which had to coincide with its neighbour. This exercise alone took us at least a day to complete. The number eight frame was also the transom, which could be fastened to it before the frame was set up.

We next came to the stempost, fore apron and hog. These were all jointed together as shown on the plans then laid as a completed unit on top of the frames, already notched out to receive the hog and fastened with galvanised bolts. The gunwales and stringers were likewise notched into the frames none of which he found particularly difficult, but at this point we made a mistake. Each chine was actually in greenheart as stated whereas the plans had called for mahogany, which is far less heavy and dense. There is often a price to be paid when departing from well established plans and we duly paid it, for the design naturally had a sharp curve towards the bow and our chines had to conform to this which they simply would not do. Our initial mistake was to fasten them at the stern end first of all, then work towards the bow, but in doing it this way we were given no leverage to bend the chines around the curve. He designed an ingenious method of pulling both chines equally so as not to push the framework out of shape, but still they would not go. We then took them off and started at the bows instead in order to gain the valuable leverage and were this time able to exert more power, but still we could not get the radius. We took them off again and tried bending using steam, and again failed due to our not being used to the technique at that time. It was at this point that desperation began to set in for we seemed to be beaten and could think of nothing beyond scrapping the old chines and ordering afresh in mahogany.

So often in life the first solution to a problem is not always the best, when with careful thought a second or even third answer will come along much better than the first. This was the case with us for my father had a brainwave. He sent the chines back to the sawmill and had them cut vertically down the middle for perhaps ten feet of their length and on their return bound the end of the sawcut temporarily with wire. We bent the first section round and secured it, followed by a sliver of greenheart the same thickness as the sawcut and glued this in place, then finally bending and glueing the second section. This method gave us a very strong build-up, in effect it was a glued laminate, and thus we were able to give our undivided attention to other things.

After the butt straps had been put in place, the next job was to fit the plywood bottom and sides where we found that the best way was to make a template in light timber, pinned temporarily to the framework with braces across the corners in order to prevent movement of the template out of shape. We would then lay it on a sheet of plywood and mark around the outline, afterwards trying the template on the job again to make sure that nothing had moved.

We progressed with glueing and screwing the ply panels and in so doing the object of our attention slowly began to look more like a boat. Eventually we came to fitting the keel with its long galvanised bolts, then finally the keel band, which extended aft to support the rudder when fitted.

The boat was now ready to be turned over and although this seemed to be a big job at the outset, it was soon accomplished. We simply approached the foreman of a nearby building site who organised about a dozen of his workforce and made an easy job of it between them. A cradle had been ready prepared and the men settled the hull onto this, but the final levelling still had to be done. In order to do this my father used the datum marks as already mentioned and brought them all to the same level.

With the hull now right way up and levelled, the task now before us lay in preparing for the engine itself by boring the sterntube through and fitting the engine beds. The gruelling job of doing

The First NIPPY

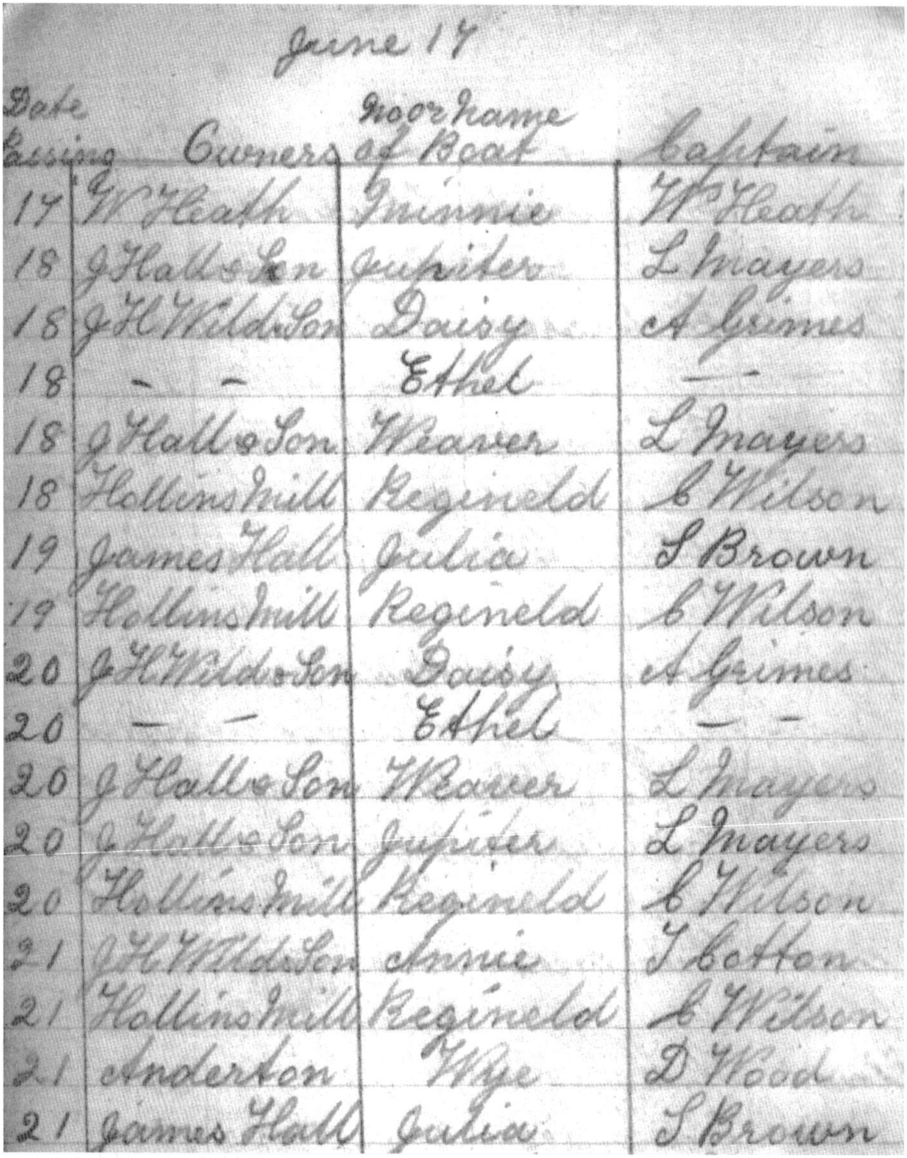

June 17

Date Passing	Owners	No or Name of Boat	Captain
17	W Heath	Minnie	W Heath
18	J Hall & Son	Jupiter	L Mayers
18	J H Wild & Son	Daisy	A Grimes
18	— —	Ethel	— —
18	J Hall & Son	Weaver	L Mayers
18	Hollins Mill	Reginald	C Wilson
19	James Hall	Julia	S Brown
19	Hollins Mill	Reginald	C Wilson
20	J H Wild & Son	Daisy	A Grimes
20	— —	Ethel	— —
20	J Hall & Son	Weaver	L Mayers
20	J Hall & Son	Jupiter	L Mayers
20	Hollins Mill	Reginald	C Wilson
21	J H Wild & Son	Annie	T Cotton
21	Hollins Mill	Reginald	C Wilson
21	Anderton	Wye	D Wood
21	James Hall	Julia	S Brown

Extract from canal records held by author showing flour traffic from the Hollinwood Branch to the Trent & Mersey with a back load of soda ash to the Ashton main line in 1928

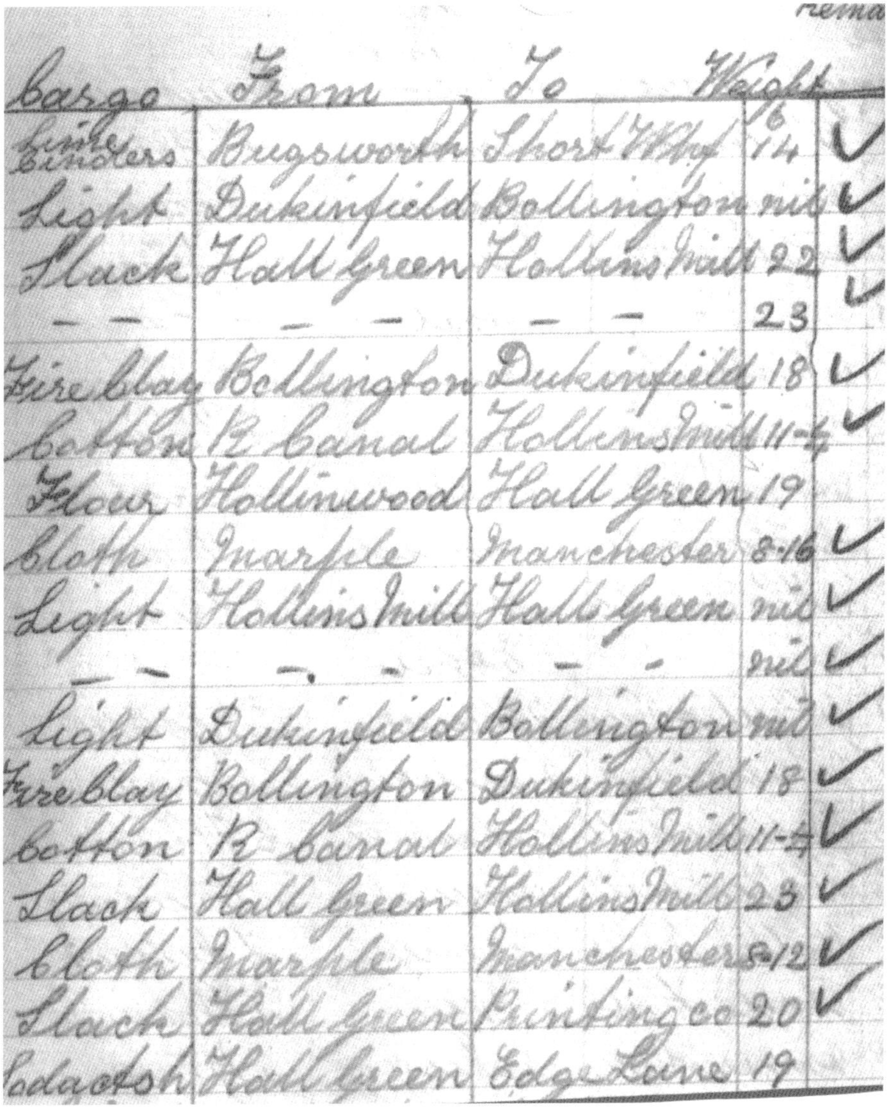

Cargo	From	To	Weight	rema
Lime Cinders	Bugsworth	Short Whf	14 6	✓
Light	Dukinfield	Bollington	nil	✓
Slack	Hall Green	Hollins Mill	22	✓
— —	— —	— —	23	✓
Fire Clay	Bollington	Dukinfield	18	✓
Cotton	R Canal	Hollins Mill	11-½	✓
Flour	Hollinwood	Hall Green	19	
Cloth	Marple	Manchester	8-16	✓
Light	Hollins Mill	Hall Green	nil	✓
— —	— —	— —	nil	✓
Light	Dukinfield	Bollington	nil	✓
Fire Clay	Bollington	Dukinfield	18	✓
Cotton	R Canal	Hollins Mill	11-½	✓
Slack	Hall Green	Hollins Mill	23	✓
Cloth	Marple	Manchester	8-12	✓
Slack	Hall Green	Printing Co	20	✓
Soda Ash	Hall Green	Edge Lane	19	

Records given to the Boat Museum, Ellesmere Port (www.thewaterwaystrust.co.uk)

The Second NIPPY on launching day

the sterntube had been made easier for us because the keel had been made up in two parts with the joint along the centreline of the sterntube and the hole machined out, so we only had to continue it through the hog and shaftlog. One reason why my father had decided not to convert a lifeboat was because of the horrific tales told about difficulties encountered when boring the sterntube, of boring into fastenings, of finding rot and finally of getting seriously out of line with the hole. In fact the only problem we had was in the opening of the sterntube joint, despite the full weight of our boat bearing down upon it, which only serves to prove that timber will move if it wants to. He solved this by boring out a series of blind holes along the line of the joint then plugging these, before boring and plugging in between and overlapping the first and so we had a watertight joint that never moved again.

Moving along to the engine beds, we first carried the centreline through using a length of string tightened through the sterntube and up to the bows, from which it was possible to set out the engine beds using dimensions taken from the engine itself standing by the boat awaiting its turn. The motive power was in fact a four horsepower Stuart Turner two stroke with magneto ignition, which despite its small output, proved to be a really heavy little beast when we came to put it in, or rather my father did since I was of little help here. When setting out solid mounted engine beds it is always a good idea to allow a little tolerance for shimming up level. In addition, we had used angle iron above and below the timbers, each with another angled piece fastened on which acted as the actual bed. From this we carried on with fitting the hanging knees, the deck beams, carlings and so on before preparing to fit the deck.

We then met with a setback. My father had a rather nasty accident at work, which stopped progress on the boat for many months and effectively thrust me into my own resources. The task of helping to build our craft had taken a good deal of spare time, which had caused me to drift away from my schoolmates, and I became rather solitary but in the end adapted to it. I took my bike and covered many miles of the local towpaths, for although the Ashton is only about six and a half miles long, it did have some lengthy branches well worth exploring. One was the Stockport Level, which ran from a junction in Openshaw between locks ten and eleven. By that time it was navigable only for the first mile or so up to the canal depot in Gorton but soon became unnavigable after that. I would have loved to see around the place but never found an excuse to enter this extensive yard with its reputation for good workmanship. Some boat or other could nearly always be seen in the short arm leading to it presumably awaiting repair, for there was said to be a well equipped dry dock.

The summit level of the Ashton is only short. It begins above Fairfield Top Lock to end in Stalybridge where it meets the Huddersfield Narrow, which climbs from here up into the Pennines with its abundant water supply.

Water and the provision of it is of prime importance to any engineer when contemplating the building of a canal. The average narrow lock needs around 25,000 gallons in order to fill it and this exercise is repeated many times a day on a busy waterway. The Ashton is fortunate in this respect since it receives its supply not only from the Huddersfield Narrow but also from the Peak Forest which it joins in Ashton. Reservoirs are of course the best known method of supplying water. However an additional source consists of rainwater falling upon higher ground adjacent to the waterway, which then percolates through.

Another branch began just above Fairfield Locks, starting with a gradual turn to the left. This was the Hollinwood Branch of around four and a half miles in length, which was joined by yet another branch, the Fairbottom at Waterhouses. This was also the site of a most intriguing flight of locks consisting of two ordinary locks with a staircase in between, being in this case two lock chambers directly connected together. There was also an ancient beam engine for returning lockage water. At one time a great volume of coal had come down here to feed the growing city but this had gradually passed over to road and later the branch had fallen into disuse owing to subsidence, but the locks and pumping engine were still more or less intact when I first saw them. One of the last traffics to travel upon it was flour with more of this in chapter four.

Fairfield Junction had been locally known as the headquarters of one James Hall who owned around a dozen craft, two being named after his daughters Maud and Ivy. He was also tenant landlord of a waterside pub 'The Waterman Inn' and so ran two businesses in successful combination. The pub survived him for some years and was still standing when I came to know the area. The broad sweep of water outside its doors, the mellowed brickwork of Bensons Mill opposite all gave the junction an indefinable atmosphere, which no architect could create. A crude wall had been thrown across the entrance to the branch when last I was there and the atmosphere quite gone.

And what about the man himself? I hope that some day his story will be told, of boats owned and of loads carried. No such account can ever tell the whole tale no matter how well researched, for without knowing the people involved we can only write of what could have been, what might have been, but not about what was.

One company director at the time was Mr Arthur Sharp, who as it happened owned a boat, which was kept at High Lane on the Macclesfield Canal, in company with his elder brother formerly a naval commander. We were invited aboard his craft the ULASS for a day trip, finding her very similar to the one we were building. It was interesting to look her over and to see the way in which she had been designed so as to make use of the limited space available. Commander Sharp made us very welcome, with many stories of his life at sea. Listening to him it was easy to see why the Royal Navy was, and I hope still is, a force to be reckoned with.

Then came the bombshell. In 1955 came shocking news of a bill before Parliament to abandon 771 miles of canal immediately with a further 994 miles to be 'retained for the present', or in other words the closure of most of the canal system as we know it today. The proposal for this came from the Board of Survey of the British Transport Commission who operated the nationalised waterways through their offshoot British Transport Waterways. The bill first emerged in the Easter of that year and was due to be put before Parliament around November, however, the commission announced that it had already decided to adopt the recommendations made and there was much talk of 'cutting out the dead wood'.

The main opposition to this came from the Inland Waterways Association and especially from its co-founder the late Robert Aickman. All through that summer the matter was most ably laid before the public by people such as John Betjemen, the poet, also the naturalist Peter Scott and the author and playwright A P Herbert. The matter received extensive television coverage, whilst in addition the press began to sit up and take a sympathetic interest. In the event this proposal was drastically reduced, and in the end sought the closure of only 90 miles, most of which consisted of the Kennet and Avon. The chairman of BTC then announced the establishment of an independent enquiry into the future of the inland waterways, which became known as the Bowes report after its chairman. Meanwhile there were various arguments ranged against the IWA in the wake of their victory. One being that retaining the waterways could adversely affect the wages of railwaymen, also that the British truck making industry could be affected if canal transport made a comeback. Self-justification came from the BTC who claimed that they had merely desired to transfer ownership of the waterways to somebody else, but as Aickman wrote 'abandonment' was the word that came first.

British Transport Waterways were only interested in transport as their name implied. They considered the great bulk of waterways to be redundant for this purpose, or nearly so. Their aim was to close down or transfer ownership to somebody else – anybody – everything except those estuarial arms where large tonnages were being carried and on which they could concentrate their resources.

The authorities were said not to like Aickman's confrontational style, which in the circumstances cannot be all that surprising since he had prevented them from causing serious mischief to the inland waterways of this country. He was not a compromiser, he believed in keeping all of the canals open, not just the pretty ones or those with a commercial future but in maintaining the system as a whole. He went against the strong tide of official opinion, which is never an easy thing to do, and dragged the IWA along with him. We attended dinners and meetings where he spoke but did not really know him nor did many people in the organisation. We exchanged letters occasionally and became disenchanted with him for a while over the Ashton. He seemed to know people of persuasion yet made mistakes, as we all do, but if any one person could be said to have influenced events on our waterways in modern times, then it would have to be him.

A great cloud of uncertainty still hung over the canals, which remained for some years, and the trauma that attended these events left us wondering if we were wasting our time in building a boat at all. It was my first encounter with those destructive forces which have afflicted the canals for so long, and it would not be my last. "Will there be any system left to cruise on when the boat is finished?" we thought, but with construction well advanced and my father now recovered we started work again. Sometimes my Uncle Bill would come along to lend a helping hand since he too was interested in boats. He worked on the Manchester Docks, which were very active then and he would tell me of his daily life there, including the loading of craft off the inland waterways, long narrow boats with cargo destined for the Midlands perhaps, or so called short boats off the Leeds & Liverpool with traffic going further north.

Steadily the work progressed yet we were surprised at the length of time it took. We had imagined that once the hull had been completed, turned over and the engine installed the rest would be easy, but in the event we were as long fitting the decks, cabin work and interior as in building the hull itself. We also encountered a kind of flat spot from time to time in which there would be a falling away of incentive and the task would become laborious. As all boatbuilders will know, the real job lies in overcoming problems as they arise, the solution to one problem only leading to the start of another or sometimes to more than one. Boatbuilding is not for the impatient or for those with little spare time. Family commitment is another ingredient to be sought before the job is started and the intending boatbuilder would do well to remember that not all projects are taken through to completion by the person who began the task. Nowadays of course a complete shell can be bought in steel or fibreglass, which cuts out half of the work.

The snows of winter passed and in the first glint of early spring the motor cruiser lay completed except for the varnish and paint. We left this to a foreman painter named Frank, or 'Bob-on' as he would often be known, since he used this term to encourage more activity from his men. Sometimes certain well-dressed individuals would visit us and I know they were from senior management. On one such visit my father mentioned the subject of actually getting the craft to the launching site nearly a mile away. "No problem, Jim," they told him, "leave it to us", and everything was arranged.

On the launching day itself we only had to find some bunting and a bottle of champagne, for the works did the rest. A job number was issued to the lifting department who then took part in proceedings. I visited their yard and noticed the amount of equipment they had. "If we don't have it, then it doesn't exist," grunted their foreman, busily directing his men. Firstly they jacked up the boat, still in its building cradle, until a railway bogie could be pushed underneath. Then it was manoeuvred across the floor until finally the bogie located into lines running through the warehouse, for most of the materials used were received by rail. Both bogie and boat were then shoved along into the open and along the track until a crane could reach them and here our craft was lifted onto a flat truck with locomotive attached and lashed securely down. We left them to bring it through the internal railway system and went ahead to the launching site where a sizeable crowd had already gathered. I was rather taken aback by this and can remember hoping that all would be well and that she would actually float.

We waited impatiently until finally she came into view. They struggled with the points which led to the canal side for this line had not been used in many years, and with a protesting squeal of wheels around the sharp curve, she was shunted under the yard crane already in position. The boat looked smaller now out in the open but with its coloured bunting, glossy paintwork and varnish gleaming in the sun, it looked an absolute picture as though we had just bought it at the boat show. The lifting gang hooked the crane on and spread the wires well padded at strategic points to avoid damaging the hull. Up she went in the air, swivelled in the right direction followed by our moment of truth.

The craft dangled just over the water with her bows positioned so that Mr Sharp could do the honours with our bottle of champagne. He named her NIPPY, then after reciting the traditional blessing smote her soundly on the stempost with the champagne. The bright frothy liquid cascaded over the stem in a tide, which then ran into the canal accompanied by a great cheer from most of the crowd, which had swelled considerably, and with an audible groan from the rest. I have built and launched boats myself since then and made it a practice to have about half the champagne splashed over the bows with the other half going down the throats of those most connected with its building, for they deserve it after all.

Down she went into the water although it seemed a shame to put such a resplendent thing into the Ashton Canal, which was not too well maintained at that time, being dreadfully weedy and murky, not at all the place for a bright pleasure boat. I noticed several members of management looking at the surface and muttering to each other. They used the canal extensively for industrial water supply but were not impressed by its condition.

We scrambled aboard as soon as she floated, checked the bilges in order to see what was happening, which to my relief were perfectly dry and so we could relax and enjoy the moment. Our only real problem came when we tried to start the engine for it steadfastly refused any attempt to coax it into life. Retrospectively, we realised that it would have been better to have taken a water supply to the inlet and given it a run whilst still ashore, but too late now. Our plan to roar away from the bank with a surge of power did not quite work out. Eventually and with some adjustment it did start, not with a surge of power but modestly as befits a four horsepower engine.

Many willing hands prepared the nearby lock for us to enter and we sailed in, which was for me an exhilarating experience to cap an eventful day. Down we went in the dripping chamber as the deep lock emptied until finally the heavy gates could be swung. Released, we slid down a canal rather less weedy, and past offices with open windows where smiling faces were everywhere. Onwards and under the towpath bridge, into the little arm where I had recently cut the weed so as to give us a clear passage up to the jetty by the house, where finally she was moored. What a day it had been!

"A Canal At Work"
by
Edward Paget-Tomlinson

"A Scene on the Trent & Marsey near Hassal Green"
During the Fifties

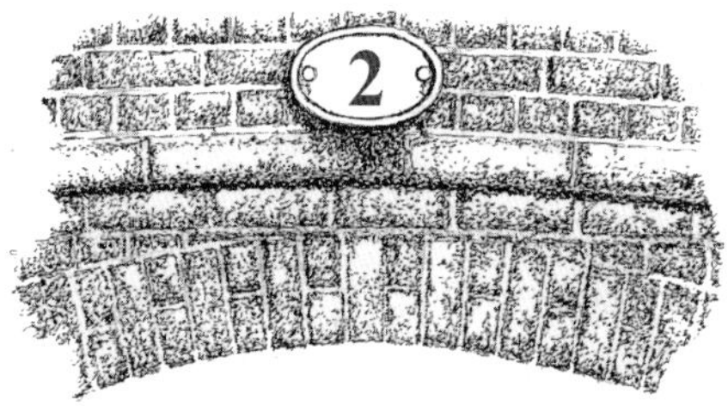

Maiden Cruise

A day or so later we cruised the short distance down to Mill Street Lock in order to have a chat with Walter, where all was affability and light, for of course we had a cruising licence which made all the difference in Walter's world. We also met his ever-cheerful wife who told us that she had been born and bred on the boats and in looking back I wish that I had asked her more about it. We really wished to make arrangements with Walter that he should accompany us on our maiden cruise or as far as the top lock anyway and he immediately accepted.

Our first destination was to be Marple, twelve miles and eleven locks away where we hoped to cruise and return over the course of Easter Holiday 1956. The only written guide we had was to all intents and purposes a reprint of the famous Bradshaw's Canal Guide first published in 1908. We made preparations to leave soon after dawn, but despite the early hour my father's mate had walked two miles and stood waiting on the bank in order to see us off. We winded with difficulty in the narrow reedy channel then sailed to the junction with the mainline where Walter awaited us. He carried with him an implement that I had often noticed in the rack outside his cottage. It had a heavy wooden shaft, maybe eleven or twelve feet long, and at the end something akin to a strong gardening fork but with the tines extended and bent at right angles. He dropped it on the boat. "What is it?" I asked. "It's a sill rake," he said and set off along the towpath ahead of us. I noticed an odd looking implement threaded through his belt as he hurried along and wondered what it could be.

We came to the first lock numbered eight in the flight and with the gates standing conveniently open sailed right in, the exhaust note now booming in the empty chamber. Walter shut the bottom gates then moved swiftly to the top end, calling down as he did so and telling us where to position the boat a few yards from the bottom end. He toiled away at the paddles and water surged powerfully into the chamber, driving us backwards so that we had to engage forward then reverse gear as the incoming flood bounced back off the gates. Experimentally we moved her a little further up the lock and discovered that actually there was a strong undertow drawing us towards the top sill. We settled back gratefully to the spot Walter had indicated and found it the best place to be for a small craft. Eventually, all the top paddles were raised with the lock filling a good deal more quickly than I had thought. The last vital drops swirled in as we all set our backs to swinging the top gate open then out she sailed all serene, with froth at the bow as though we had launched her again with champagne.

We sailed along to the next lock at Clayton Lane where I nipped ashore in order to give Walter a hand. Climbing the stone steps, I noticed how well worn they were and that I was by no means the first to use them. We were a new boat on a very old canal and I felt comfortable with the thought somehow. Closing the bottom gates we moved to the top end and I realised the purpose of the implement he carried for it was of course a windlass. He taught me always to lift the ground paddles first. "Never lift the gate paddles until the water is over the sill", he told me, "or the boat could be flooded". Other lessons were always to set the safety catch before lifting the paddle. Never to leave a windlass on a lifted paddle and to wind the paddle down with a windlass or run it gradually down with the hand as a brake but never to let it drop freely.

On again we moved, rising up through the levels on this quiet Easter morning, for the hour was still early with nobody else about. To our right stood the works of the English Steel Corporation, although formerly those of Armstrong Whitworth, battleship builders of renown and employers of my grandfather who had been a foundry foreman there. At this site the gun barrels would be made and the massive buildings, brooding and silent now, would once be vibrant in clangour and flame both by day and night as the mighty barrels were cast and trepanned, rifled, sleeved and sent to the ships under construction at Barrow-in-Furness.

Still we sailed on until nearing Crabtree Lane where the surroundings were quite open with easy access to the canal side, and it was here that we ran into problems, for a pair of gates could not be closed together due to obstructions in the gatewell where the gates operated. Walter had to position the boat slightly behind the sill and here the long rake came into play. Balancing on the bows, cap on back of head and Woodbine between lips, he tweaked out each obstruction with dextrous ability until finally the gates could be fairly shut. We had the same problem at the next lock, twice more after that and on one of these episodes we nearly lost Walter. The boat had grounded in the shallows below a lock entrance and we all were pushing and pulling valiantly in order to free it. Walter shuffled along a narrowing stone ledge till he could reach her, and then he gave a mighty shove.

His plan must have been to hop aboard as soon as she moved. Unfortunately he literally missed the boat for it set off into the lock leaving him perched with just his heels on the narrowing ledge and nothing but the canal before him. Although an Ashton enthusiast I have never been keen to enter it's far from limpid waters and the same applied to poor Walter, judging by the expression on his face. He kept himself pinned against the wall, which luckily battered outwards and gingerly ventured a hand aloft. "Pull me up," he whispered. We did just that and our lock keeper breathed again. The obstructions had delayed us and now there were a number of people about, curious to see a boat on this little used waterway, many being youths who flung bricks etc into the water and generally made a nuisance of themselves although nothing serious, unlike today. "Push off," Walter would say to them with a baleful glare. Most took one look at him and went but some did not appear to understand, and he would clatter them around the ear, and they understood.

Being still a callow youth, I imagined that most canal travel must be the same but in fact the one on which we so blithely sailed was notorious among the boating public for being difficult to negotiate. Many boatowners gave it a wide berth, the few attempting passage tended to write articles about it afterwards and were even given the occasional prize, all of which we were blissfully unaware at the time.

The rubbish dumping tailed off before we reached Edge Lane Lock, probably due to a lock keeper being resident there, although I cannot remember his name. Afterwards we came to the longish length before the final two locks are reached. Part way along was the works of Carrington Sellers who clearly had made heavy use of the canal at one time since the place itself was laid out in favour of canal transport. There were Lancashire boilers positioned within yards of the bank, which consisted of one continuous wharf along the offside. Numerous craft were sunk including dayboats with which I was already familiar. Birmingham is always regarded as being the home of the dayboat but they were certainly used elsewhere.

Trudging on beside Walter, I learned something of the history surrounding this waterway and of the Peak Forest and Macclesfield for they became joined together as a result of being taken over by a railway company many years ago. The Ashton was considered to be the most important because a great deal of traffic either went to or came from its many wharves and warehouses, also for its busy collieries in addition to a railway interchange point. It had been the centre of administration with the offices at Gorton. This had ended following nationalisation and the Peak Forest and the Macc were now a single section controlled by the canal depot at Marple whilst the Huddersfield Narrow had come under the control of Gorton.

I also began to learn some of the terminology used by canalmen that is often different from correct engineering terminology. For example, strictly speaking the correct term for a stretch of water between locks is a 'pound', yet I never heard Walter or any other canalman on the Ashton, Peak Forest or Macc describe it as being anything other than a 'pond'. It should also be noted that there is no standard terminology in use throughout the canals not even on the narrow canals. Later I gained access to lock keepers records of long ago and it became obvious that this use of terms was not recent affectation. Older hands taught the new recruits, which also applied to myself, when starting work on the canals many years later and I use this perhaps rather outdated vocabulary since it is what I am most comfortable with.

Continuing on we came to Copperas Lane Swingbridge where my other grandfather worked at a blacksmith's shop, mostly shoeing horses and treating them when they were sick, for he was also a farrier or horse doctor. My mother remembers taking medicines to stables in the area and it is possible that he would have looked after the boat horses since there must have been a good number hauling the loads of coal, ashes, chemicals and cotton in that hard but simple world. So we came to the final two locks, which once were twinned in order to cope with the traffic and now lifted us up to the summit level at Fairfield Junction Wharf where we said goodbye to Walter. He arranged to meet us again here at 1pm the following day.

The main line continues with a bend to the right which is deceptively sharp and according to legend it was at this spot many years ago that a horse, pulling at right angles to the boat, succeeded in capsizing it with its top heavy load of mast high laden cotton bale.

Stowing the windlasses away, we settled back in some relief, for the locks had been hard work. We followed the canal as it meandered through Droylsden, Audenshaw and Guide Bridge before finally reaching Ashton and its junction with the Peak Forest. A sizeable warehouse stood opposite with the remains of a waterwheel in a pit which used to drive the machinery. A canal house was situated at the corner whilst a lovely stone bridge carried the towpath onwards to a junction with the Huddersfield Narrow.

The Peak Forest starts just after an aqueduct over the Tame, which actually belongs to the

Ashton. Immediately afterwards there was an arm leading off which I am told once had a dry dock located somewhere on it. There next came a large earthenware pottery works, which like the arm and house has now gone. In approaching the junction we had sailed up one side of the Tame and having crossed were now travelling down the other.

Onwards through Dukinfield we travelled, towards Hyde and passing another canal arm before we reached there. Then came a large mill belonging to Ashton Brothers with its boiler house adjacent to the canal that at one time was served by the boats of James Hall. A proud firm this, judging by a sign outside the offices in Manchester declaring 'Ashton Brothers Stronghold'. A firm with the same family name features in a classic 'The Manchester Man' by Mrs Linnaeus Banks, which tells a compelling story of life in the old city including the Peterloo Massacre. Soon afterwards there was a winding hole by Hyde wharf and warehouse, this was small and quaint with a projecting veranda giving shelter to the craft which once used it. Beautifully proportioned in stone and giving satisfaction to behold.

Hyde tended to show an industrial side to the canal, yet suddenly we were through and into open countryside, the first to be seen on the trip. I kept a sharp look out ahead for the guidebook said that the first of two tunnels awaited us, sure enough we rounded a turn with ground rising on either side and there it was, the tunnel bore much smaller that I had anticipated. We entered slowly, our feeble light hardly reflecting off the constricting walls and although we were careful, we could not avoid scraping some varnish off during the passage through. Woodley Tunnel is only 176 yards in length, though it had seemed much longer. Out into the daylight again and onward through countryside dotted with houses, we came to pleasant Romiley and it was here that a tragedy had once occurred, by a small overspill weir to be seen on the right.

Two horse-drawn craft once met a this point and naturally one had to give way to the other in accordance with the rules, easing the towline so that the right of way craft could sail over it without hindrance. However, it was and still is the practice with wooden craft to have strips of metal known as shoeing fastened to the bottom planks near the edge to protect against wear. One of these must have become loose and hung down. The slack towline became wedged in this causing a strong pull backwards. Unfortunately, the mast towing pin was fixed in place unlike the 'modern' type, which can swivel back in case this happens. Something had to give and so it was that the horse was pulled backwards and sideways, fell into the canal and took its young attendant with it. He was unfortunately drowned.

So to the second tunnel, Hyde Bank – 308 yards long, which this time had no towpath and is of wider bore. Once again we entered the darkness and were not alone for there were bats in this unfrequented place. None of us liked canal tunnels really. The countryside now became more spectacular; a deep valley lay to one side with trees standing high, dappled in the spring sunshine. There next came the site of the old Rose Hill tunnel, now opened out, and then beyond that the Marple Aqueduct itself.

This consisted of a triple arch span high over the Goyt, which with its design and blend of stonework ingrained with the patina of years, made the structure appear as if somehow it had grown there. The trough is hardly wider than the width of a boat, which caused trouble during the days of horse towage. The sudden surge of water from the deep locks of Marple not far away could drive an approaching craft backwards, especially if she were loaded and so compromise the horse. For this reason and in order to overcome it, rings were set into the stonework at regular intervals along the offside so that in such circumstances the boater could take a turn and wait for the flood to subside. The aqueduct has since been rebuilt and the rings are no longer to be seen. This we passed, dizzy with the height of it, and so as evening approached we arrived at our destination, the bottom of Marple Locks. I visited this spot again recently to note with satisfaction that little had changed. There is still the wide sweep of towpath, the magnificence of the locks to one side and a stone bridge without towpath to the other, seeming to make the mooring private somehow. There are still a good many tall trees around, and trains still snake across the valley on a viaduct higher than the canal, although they are no longer steam. We slept peacefully that night to the quiet murmurings of the byewash opposite.

Came the morning and our first breakfast on board was at hand, the technology being refreshingly simple. It consisted of two methylated spirit camping type cookers on a tray, which we used without improvement for years. Our boat attracted several early morning strollers since the sight of a boat here must have been a rare event at that time.

Breakfast finished we turned around to set off for home and our appointment with Walter. The journey back was completed without incident and NIPPY arrived above Fairfield Lock at ten minutes before the appointed time. Walter was also punctual and the descent to Clayton started immediately. We sailed through the locks with very little trouble due to having cleared the gates on the previous day. We parted company with Walter at the entrance to our little arm, and as we said goodbye he handed us a windlass, which has since travelled over many waterways. There is to be found stamped into it the initials of the Great Central Railway. And so ended the maiden voyage of NIPPY, which I always look back upon with pleasure.

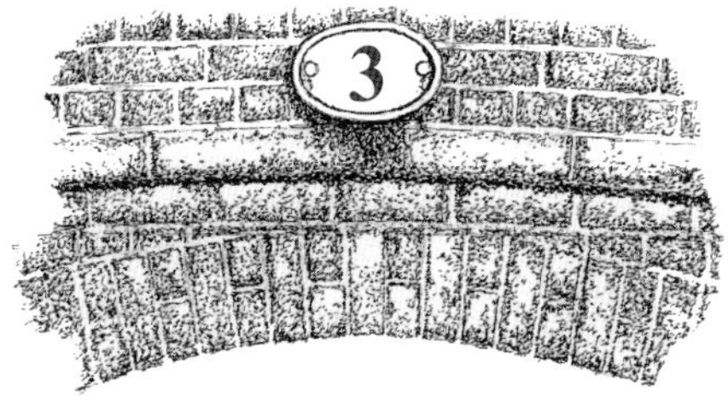

To Lincoln

That spring and summer we sailed up and down the Ashton, sometimes accompanied by the relations. Being members of the IWA, we knew that their annual rally was to be held at Lincoln, which involved using the tidal Trent. Nowadays with much more experience the knowledge of this would cause me to pause and think, to make enquiries and to lay plans. In the event we asked nobody, we simply upped and went.

I forget now if the long-suffering Walter accompanied us up the locks, but at any rate we arrived at the top with very little trouble. It is often said that a person remembers the weather in his early days as being usually fine, but August 1956 was for me one of the wettest I can ever remember. There were few days when it did not rain convincingly and especially as we approached a flight of locks. Against this we each wore a plastic pacamac, which in the unusual exertion of lifting paddles and hauling on balance beams proved to have the strength and durability of gossamer. As the trip progressed we were to meet other crews in the same attire.

The locks done we set off again towards Ashton and then onto the Lower Peak Forest through now familiar country towards Hyde, and it was here that we ran into problems for we were into late summer and the weed had grown in earnest. It clogged around the screw causing us to reverse several times in order to throw it off. We had bought a two-bladed propeller designed to cut weed, or so it was said, but this forecast proved optimistic in the event and there was a noticeable vibration at times even with the prop unimpeded by weed. A maintenance boat blocked our progress, AGNES I think she was called. “Bit weedy round here,” I said to a member of the crew who emerged briefly at the door but did not reply. Eventually the weed cleared and we sailed on through better water to the bottom of Marple Locks where once again we moored.

The incessant rain awoke us the following morning in good time for breakfast, and then we

Waterways past and present with the journeys of NIPPY shown in bold lines (illustrated by Edward Paget-Tomlinson)

tackled this deep flight of locks. Their standard of construction is not really of the best, which is a pity since the technique of building locks was well established by the time they were done. The pound lock is thought to be an Italian invention where a canal was built in order to carry stone for the building of a cathedral in Milan.

An earlier type was known as a flash lock used on the ancient river navigations. In this case the river would be narrowed at the selected point and a gate installed. This would normally be left in the closed position, causing the water to back up so that a barge could float over the shallows further upstream. Naturally, the paddles would have to be drawn so that the gate could be swung for a barge to pass through and it was this dropping of the river level which created a great deal of bitterness between the barge owner and millers, who needed a constant head of water in order to turn their waterwheels.

The locks at Marple are remarkable for the way in which they were surveyed and levelled. Every lock is more or less of the same great depth all the way up this impressive flight. In filling a lock, we would first lift the ground paddles and later on the gate paddles, or dandy paddles as they are called on the Peak Forest. Onwards to the top where we rounded the junction with the Macclesfield. This begins with the site of a former stop lock known as 'New Lock' by canalmen, since it was built a few years after the flight.

We tied for a while at the canal depot just ahead of the former Grand Union narrow boat ARIES, recently docked at Gorton and resplendent in her livery of dark blue and yellow, she must have been one of the last craft to be repaired there.

After taking on provisions, water and petrol, we set off along the Macclesfield Canal where everything before us was unexplored territory as far as we were concerned and most certainly a new experience for us, all the way to Lincoln many miles away. The engine's water circulating pump proved to be troublesome on occasion due to lifting a head of water almost up to its capacity. The flow could sometimes die away completely following inevitable fluctuations in the trim of the boat, leaving us with scalding hot water turning to steam. Luckily it did not happen often, but I remember us stopping in some attractive and isolated spot somewhere along the Macc in order to deal with it.

The Macclesfield Canal is a good example of late canal engineering with fine embankments and lovely stone bridges. The canal itself is rather shallow with the banks badly eroded from the wash of many powered craft including coal traffic to Marple from Stoke. It was built with the gentle wash of horse towage in mind, not that of the savage screw. However, there turned out to be ample draught for us as we sailed towards evening on its placid waters.

Nearing Bollington we saw a greenish white cone atop a hill in the distance. "What's that?" we enquired of somebody, trudging resolutely along the rain sodden towpath. "White Nancy," he replied with scarcely a pause. We later found out that it had been erected to commemorate the Battle of Waterloo. Next came a bridge carrying Sugar Lane, which intersects the canal at an awkward angle, causing the bridge to be built on the skew. Travelling slowly we had plenty of time to admire this perfection of the stonemason's art. After that followed a little wharf where clay was once loaded, then the vast bulk of Clarence Mill, a vision of Victorian confidence in every set of stone. Soon afterwards the land fell abruptly away and we were sailing on an embankment, soaring high above the town. Here it was that we paused awhile before deciding to stay there overnight with the lights of Bollington far below.

The next day turned out to be very fine which we were determined to enjoy since it had been rather wet so far. There were several swing bridges to negotiate between Bollington and Macclesfield, the next town on our route, and in fact there were quite a number on the Macclesfield and Peak Forest at that time. These varied considerably in the ease with which they could be swung. Being timber, I suspect that they tended to warp according to the weather, but there was a lack of simple maintenance where the grooves in which the ball bearings turned needed to be flushed out with water every so often. Someone we knew actually carried a block and tackle for shifting the more stubborn ones.

And so it was that Macclesfield came into view. Not impressively as Bollington had done, but more gradually as befits a larger town. The town really began at bridge 36, known to canal folk as 'Spikey Bridge' whatever the official name might be.

We passed Buxton Road Wharf with several boathouses situated on it before going under the bridge to find large buildings beyond. The carrier John Green had once been based here, mostly taking coal from Stoke-on-Trent to Marple, which had only ceased a year or two before. His craft had been docked at Braunston on the Grand Union where a high standard of repair and decoration could be guaranteed. He still lived at that time in a canal-side cottage nearby.

Onwards through Macclesfield and out into the countryside once again, we passed through peaceful Oakgrove Valley with its mass of tall shady trees. I have since travelled along in the spring where in places it has been carpeted with a mass of bluebells, most colourful to behold.

We came eventually to the top of Bosley Locks, although the last mile or two had seemed to take an age due to the shallow water. We noticed the rather odd looking stone cottage at the top of the flight which has since been rebuilt. There was no external water supply laid on so I went instead to the cottage door and operated the bell push. No bell rang but a light flashed within the premises and a charming old lady, Mrs Wood, who was rather deaf came to the door and filled our cans for us, remarking on how well they looked. This done we started down the flight. They proved to be lighter than at Marple with the top gates being paired, which is most unusual for narrow locks. The ground paddles were an absolute brute to lift and certainly not geared for the ease of the operator. They have since been replaced though examples may still be seen next to the disused sideponds.

We passed through the twelve locks without undue difficulty, but could not help noticing that some of the top gates did not fit too well. This was because they were hung in the same manner as the bottom gates. These were allowed to hang slightly forward and relied upon water pressure to push them back against the sills. Unfortunately, with the much smaller top gates, there was not enough pressure available to do this especially when the mitres became grain bound, and a sizeable gap could be left between gates and sills through which the water poured. A knack could be employed in order to overcome this, but very few boat crews knew of it and nor did we to begin with. Many years later I became the carpenter for British Waterways on the Marple section, and my first major task was to repair the flight, which meant by that time it was in very poor condition with some of the lock ponds emptying overnight. I repaired, and in a few cases replaced some of the gates and made it so that they only needed to be put together in order to obtain a fit. We stopped early that day by the bottom of the flight and opposite a disused corrugated iron warehouse that once served a works in Bosley.

We thought we had time in hand so we made a leisurely start, but as we sailed through the loneliness of Pearsons Valley there came a serious problem. The canal ahead was covered in weed and banks of floating sedge. We ploughed into it but finally the propeller became clogged, so we had to reverse the weed off in order to try again. The weed became thicker still and eventually brought us to a halt. A weedcutter had been along and cut the stuff though it had not been removed and it now gathered in great banks as far as the eye could see. Our boathooks proved to be of little use for the purpose of poling along so there was nothing for it but to close the bank and attempt to land through the densely reeded sides. We eventually struggled ashore with towlines from fore and aft, for luckily we carried plenty of line, and set off trudging along the towpath, blessed for once by the fact that NIPPY was not a particularly large craft and easy to tow. The trouble was that the high, dense reeds made bowhauling rather difficult for there were times when only the cabin top could be seen from the bank. In addition they turned out to be the favourite place for many thousands of flies, which took to the air and winged towards us in squadrons as the towlines disturbed them, attacking with the ferocity of kamikaze pilots. I have hated the little swines ever since.

Every now and then we would come to a clear patch until eventually the canal ahead remained clear. We rejoined the boat at a bridge hole and set off with a sigh of relief, but after only a mile or so we were back to bowhauling. The sun beat down relentlessly for a change and I forget now if Humphrey Bogart had made the film 'African Queen' by that time, for parts of it could have been shot on the Macclesfield Canal saving the trouble of going into darkest Africa. My mother tended to be marooned on the boat during these occasions but kept us plied with orange drinks when we all met at a bridgehole, which put us one up on Humphrey.

So it went on. There would be a long clear patch, which tempted us to free the propeller, hanging over the stern to do so before unblocking the seacock strainer so as to start the engine and cover some distance before the next patch. Then we were brought yet again to a halt and as there was a house nearby, the occupants invited us in for a light meal. "We know how you feel," they said. "We used to have a boat on the canal". Nearing Hall Green we came across the spoon dredger TYRIAN, tied up and apparently not in use. Handing the towrope over it, I inadvertently stepped on a large gear wheel which instantly spun round, trapping my foot firmly in the cog and I was limping for a day or two afterwards. A spoon dredger worked exactly as its name suggests. A small crane was built upon a deck amidships which supported a large spoon. The crew would literally drive this into the silt and the crane would hoist it up. In fact this outmoded implement remains the only dredging plant that I remember seeing anywhere along the Ashton, Peak Forest or Macc at that time. It sank in Macclesfield some years later, and was then raised and broken up during a stoppage in Bosley Locks.

The weed eased off considerably after leaving Hall Green Stop Lock so that we made better progress, yet the weed had delayed us and the day was already well advanced when we swung onto the summit level of the Trent & Mersey, a great cross county waterway uniting the east coast with the west. A long tunnel lay not far away as we already knew. Piercing the last of the Pennine

Chain, the range of hills that divides northern England like a backbone running centrally through the land. The need for a tunnel could have been obviated altogether if the canal had been constructed a few miles further south, but the engineer suspected that vital water supplies were to be found under the hill and so it proved to be. That engineer was James Brindley, of whom more is discussed in a later chapter.

We journeyed perhaps half a mile and suddenly there it was, not one tunnel but two, for another had been built alongside the first owing to the density of traffic when the canal was at its peak. Ground subsidence had greatly affected both and the original tunnel was now closed although water coloured the deepest ochre still flowed from it. A steel profile gauge hung improbably low outside the entrance to the newer one, which we had to push aside in order to enter. We looked at it in disbelief. Surely the tunnel inside could not have settled so much? Stories came to mind of a pleasure boat, which had become well and truly stuck for many hours before being freed. Her crew then carried out drastic modifications to the superstructure with a saw and tried once more. She travelled a little further only to be stuck again and took even longer to be released. Now it was our turn to have a try. The tunnel was also said to have a ghost, a story that did little to improve our confidence as we entered the gloomy portal.

The reluctant beams of our inadequate searchlight strove to pierce the darkness ahead and we vowed yet again to replace it fairly soon. Luckily there was plenty of room at the outset so we made our way along feeling gradually emboldened. Suddenly in the light we could see that the tunnel was reduced most markedly ahead and we reduced our speed to a crawl, whilst the engine's exhaust sounded a different booming note; we cautiously entered this more restricted bore. Not too bad, we thought after a while, but then it reduced again. The continuing but useless towpath forced us against the curving brickwork and inevitably we caught the superstructure in a noisy scrape, which fortunately caused little damage. I noted that the arch had distorted due to the pressure so that the crown of it seemed flatter than it should have been. I had to keep reminding myself that I was navigating a main line commercial waterway in the middle of the twentieth century. No wonder canal transport has declined, I thought as we crept gingerly along. The vague pinprick of light at the other end took ages to enlarge, but finally we were through the most restricted section and could pick up a little speed again to head more quickly towards the exit. Finally we arrived into blessed daylight, glad that it was behind us. I should mention at this point that considerable work has been done to the tunnel since.

We now were sailing along with the industry of Stoke on either side and I looked forward expectantly to seeing working craft tied up at the various wharves, since the Trent & Mersey still carried a significant traffic at that time. I seem to remember seeing a short arm with boats at the end of it soon after leaving Harecastle, but nothing else for some time. Where are they all I wondered, then we saw a considerable fleet tied up with more ashore under a covered dockyard. This turned out to be the fleet of Mersey Weavers who were the largest carriers in the area just then. There remained barely enough room for us to pass so we slowed right down giving me plenty of time to study the craft as we eased ourselves by. Mersey Weavers themselves were painted with a red name panel but they had taken over another carrier called Andertons a year or two before, so many of these were still in their livery of black and cream. We glanced into an open engine room where an old fashioned semi diesel could be seen, burnished copper pipes gleaming slyly in the final rays of the setting sun.

Darkness was soon upon us and the searchlight came into use well before the top lock at Etruria loomed into view. Normally we would have tied up for the night since it is unsafe to negotiate locks after darkness has fallen. Our haste was due to the fact that a stoppage had been announced, commencing on the following day. Stoppage work was usually done in summertime then. Every factory in town would be closed on a particular week, often known as 'Wakes Week', for the annual holiday. The canal boats that supplied them would also stop and the engineers would seize their chance to do much needed repair work. In this case a new pair of bottom gates were to be fitted at Cockshute Lock, fourth one down the flight. We had to pass this or forget our trip to Lincoln, but soon we were through and breathed more easily. We negotiated the fifth lock and knew there would be no more for while, and here we tied up gratefully for the night. It had been a long day, yet somewhere astern another light could be seen, indicating that some other traveller was still on the move.

We awoke to find ourselves in a rocky, man-made canyon where although the traffic of Stoke roared by on a road, we felt somehow apart from it. Unmistakable railway noises also indicated the presence of a station not far away. Soon we were off for there were many miles to go and we now realised how one could be delayed due to unforeseen circumstances, so we pressed on through territory more familiar to me now but quite unknown then. Parts of the waterway broadened out as we left Stoke behind and the main thing I remember was a great flock of swans making use of it and brightening a landscape still somewhat drab in the uncertain sunlight. Working craft rarely used the canal beyond Trentham except when a stoppage elsewhere forced them to do so. The Trent & Mersey became a pleasure boat waterway from here on, and due to the much lesser numbers of such craft, it meant that we seldom met another boat. One could observe this much lighter use in the locks themselves. Overnight rain still lay in the lock gearing even towards midday, whilst a light scum had formed around the top gates indicating that nothing had been through for some time. We were now becoming used to canal travel so much so that our proficiency increased with every lock and we tackled the four at Meaford in their attractive setting with growing confidence. It was a pleasure to operate locks without having to rake the sill off first as on the Ashton and we made good progress.

The locks at Stone soon followed, then came those at Aston, Sandon, Weston and Hoo Mill as the canal became almost riverine itself, following the slow moving Trent in its broad valley, sharing it with road and rail with plenty of space for each form of transport with none encroaching upon the other.

There is something infinitely satisfying about travelling on a waterway that is well maintained as that part of the Trent & Mersey was at that particular time. The lock gates all trim in their black and white with the gearing recently oiled, each with its neat lock cottage alongside. The waterway itself being so deep and wide let us slip easily along for mile after mile, cattle gazing with gentle enquiry as we passed, and the canal so full of wildlife as it was. Waterfowl nested in the reeds, or crossed in haste at our approach. Hovering dragonflies flashed overhead whilst down below the surface rippled with the occasional rising fish. All very satisfying and it remains one of my favourite stretches to this day.

Eventually we came to the junction with the Staffordshire & Worcestershire at Great Haywood, which is another arm of the great cross, linking the Severn, Thames, Trent and Mersey. Canalmen were busily working on the fine junction bridge, pausing to watch and nodding as we passed. The view through the arch beckoned us invitingly but we left it for another day to continue on our way towards an appointment with the mighty Trent. The Trent & Mersey seems to change somewhat after Great Haywood is passed, the countryside being less open and rolling than before, with the canal itself in need of dredging, or rather it was the case then. I also noted the poor state of the banks and how they had been damaged by passing craft over the years, a problem common to many waterways and not caused simply by the advent of pleasure craft. We seemed to progress more slowly now, making it through craggy Armitage Tunnel, and as time went by the landscape saw yet another change as we brushed the edge of Cannock Chase and reached Wood End Lock. Finally, we came upon Shade House and Middle Locks, heralding Fradley Junction and our moorings for the night. We had done well that day, covering thirty miles and more, which put us back on schedule for the trip. I had a brief look at the canal yard before turning in.

The weather had been mostly kind to us over the last couple of days, but now the rain returned with a vengeance. I had planned to explore the junction in greater detail, but left it for another time since my parents wanted to be away, rain or no rain, and so off we went again. There were not only locks to negotiate but also a river as the canal shares its course with the Trent for a short distance, and we noted ruefully the masses of floating weed and debris above the downstream lock with further quantities of it already raked ashore. The only change in the rain seemed to be that it came down with even greater intensity as the day wore on. At one point, a whole line of ducks watched us disconsolately from the bank with not a honk or cackle to be heard anywhere among them. "Even the ducks are fed up," my father said, which seemed to be the case. The locks changed from narrow to wide, the first we had come across and seemingly cavernous by comparison. I could not help thinking about all the water that was being used simply to pass our little boat through but we struggled on, squelching around every lock until the canal town of Shardlow came into view as the lowering sky turned into dusk. That night another boat felt its way carefully past and we watched as his lights disappeared around the turn.

We set forth again the following morning, once more in heavy rain, only to come across our fellow traveller of the night before. It turned out to be a converted army pontoon with the poor man clearly in trouble. He remained tied up, struggling to start his outboard, fiddling with the carburettor, pulling hard on the cord then brushing the rain off it with the sleeve of his plastic mac. Behind him a gaggle of children were stood, asking questions as only children can. Slowing down, we asked solicitously, "Need any help?" He gave no answer, save that cackling cry reserved for those on the verge of insanity. Then he struck the engine a fearsome blow with his fist, subsiding into the boat, nursing his hand and cursing volubly. Help was at hand so we passed quietly on, resolving never to buy a British Anzani. Soon we had passed the final lock on the Trent & Mersey, leading us into the Trent itself. We went along a short canal section and there it was, intersecting from the right with the Derwent arriving from the left. Both rivers carried a considerable flow due to all the rain and I remember seeing a ridge formed at their confluence, not down the centre, but to one side since the Trent seemed much the stronger. We found our way to Sawley Lock and beyond there to

Cranfleet, where on the way I noticed with interest the neat entrance to the Erewash on our left and the Soar to Leicester and beyond to our right. So through Beeston Lock and back onto the quieter waters of the Nottingham Canal, which bypassed an un-navigable portion of the river. Our brief spell of river navigation had been exhilarating and I looked forward to rejoining it again soon.

Wending our way through some uninspiring areas, we tied up above Meadow Lane Lock where the lock keeper and his wife made us welcome. We stayed for a day or so to rest and to dry out, for most of our clothes were wet with no real facilities to wash and dry them on board. Whilst there, a deep laden barge came up the lock to travel slowly past, stirring up the bottom as it crept on by. "Where bound for?" I asked. "Leicester," the steerer replied before returning his full attention to keeping his charge in whatever channel there might be. I hoped that his cargo was not perishable. After our short recuperation we were once again ready to face the Trent. The lock keeper warned us about difficulties to be met with on the way to Torksey, which we tried to memorise. Everyone would be up very early on that first cruise though we grew out of the habit later, but sure enough we made yet another early departure thus giving us time in hand to tackle whatever came our way.

Trent barges lay at the wharves beyond the lock. We noted the size of them and decided to keep a keen lookout. Came the first of the massive locks where our boat seemed tiny inside and I think that it was either at this one or the next we were overhauled by one of John Harker's tankers returning empty to the coast. We engaged the crew in conversation and asked for details of any shallows on the way. "Tell you what," they said, "why not take a tow with us and we'll show you," which we did. The barge fairly thrummed along at speeds well beyond anything we could have managed and I thoroughly enjoyed it. Designed to thrust against the tide and current, deep laden with petrol, she was now riding high and empty, and with NIPPY towing like a dinghy astern she fairly belted downstream with the current under her. I took stock of our tug as we sped along. Regrettably, her name is long forgotten, but a dedication on the wheelhouse said that the craft had been found crewless and drifting off the beaches of Dunkirk some sixteen years before. I remember thinking that she at least had been lucky for there must have been many a craft never returned from that heroic episode.

Other commercial traffic was now on the move. We saw laden craft coming the other way, sometimes singly or sometimes under tow when I tried to imagine the forces at work on the steel towlines as they went by, and what would happen if the tow snapped or if it ever occurred. Must do, I decided. Sometimes our new friends would point across the water, shaking their hand vigorously, indicating shallow water over there or at a bridge show that the other arch was not navigable. We took it all in. The miles and locks went swiftly by with the only problem arising at Newark, where some tight manoeuvring was called for past several moored craft. So we came to Cromwell Lock with tidal waters at the tail of it, that twice-daily miracle of nature which we take so much for granted. Perhaps the tide was full or on the ebb for I noted no slackening in our speed towards Torksey and we had to part company to my regret. We gave them a good tip.

Torksey Lock marks the start of the Fossdyke Canal where we tied overnight. There was a variety of craft around including a fairly large motor cruiser, which we were invited to visit. Stepping aboard, we marvelled at their space and luxury – so different from our own. They had come upstream through the tidal section and told a sorry tale of how an apparently suitable mooring had turned into a nightmare experience as the tide receded and the boat canted over on a steeply shelving bank. The situation had been saved only by putting plenty of lines ashore and hoping that she would not roll right over. They had been washing off a dirty mark made by the returning tide well up the topsides of the boat. We could tell they had been very near to disaster.

The next day began with a mounting feeling of achievement for this would be the final leg of our long journey to Lincoln, with only a few miles now separating us from our goal. The canal went along wide and very straight, for our Roman conquerors constructed the Fossdyke building it originally as a drainage channel. Yet the going can become rather tedious and personally I am rather glad that it is roads and not waterways for which they were famous in this country. We made good progress though, our wake stretching out behind us as we sailed past Saxilby and so on to our destination, Brayford Pool in Lincoln to join the other craft already assembled there. The arrangements for receiving craft were not of the best so we simply found an empty space at the far corner and tied up, going ashore for a leisurely meal.

Readers should understand that national boat rallies then were by no means the spectacular events they are today, with many hundreds of craft attending, drawing crowds in their thousands and with many other side events planned. I cannot even remember seeing a marquee at Lincoln, although presumably there must have been one. We wandered happily around the city in our torn plastic macs, eating ice cream and taking in the sights. Some of the family of the Lord Mayor came aboard to see us accompanied by the press who were also very kind. Everyone attended the rally dinner where Aickman gave a purposeful speech in his own inimitable style. Everything was made clear to us, sharply black and white. To one side was the government with their agencies still plotting to shut our waterways down or at least dragging their feet. The initial threat to close a vast mileage had been parried, yet danger still remained with British Transport Waterways making no secret of the fact. On the other side were the active waterways enthusiasts, most of whom were present (and were not many) to oppose the weight of official rule. The entire story of the struggle to keep our canals open is an object lesson in how officialdom can sometimes be wrong. It was up to members to campaign for their own local waterways, I thought, and awoke from my reverie as Aickman finished his speech to great applause.

The rally over, we departed en masse, most of us heading back towards the Trent. My final memory of Brayford Pool was the sight of keels being unloaded of their bagged cargo, potatoes I think it was. The men were hard at work whipping out the spuds as we passed. Our convoy reached the lock at Torksey to be greeted by the sight of a laden Harker's tanker, thrusting resolutely upstream, her great bluff bows shouldering the river aside, all very fascinating to someone interested in waterborne trade. Several of us crammed into the lock and soon we were back amongst the tides of the Trent, this time without our friendly barge crew. We came across another barge, which was not so friendly, somewhere around Newark. She was laden with gravel so deep that the lop in the river came onto her side decks and without a substantial coaming around the hold, she would most certainly have sunk. We tried to pass in the narrow channel as everyone else had, however, the skipper must have increased the engine revs and we were drawn alongside, unable to get ahead. I leapt aboard the barge in order to fend us off and the deckhand paused in his task of sweeping back the waters off the deck with a long brush to give me a hand. A baleful glare from my father caused the skipper to ease his throttle, thus enabling us to draw ahead and join the other pleasure craft tightly packed in the lock. Once the lock had filled we all sailed out with Ray Slack in the lead, Hon Secretary for many years of the North West IWA. A sharp bend lay ahead and Ray peered around it. "Look out," he shouted, "There's a barge coming". We all scuttled to the side leaving Ray and his crew backing rapidly away from the approaching leviathan.

As time went on, the fleet became steadily more separated until finally towards dusk on the second day there was only one other craft in sight, a converted ship's lifeboat from Chester. It followed us into the final big lock on the river, and by the time we had passed through, it was quite dark. We resisted the temptation to stay in the lock entrance overnight. There could be barges on the move by the following morning and we did not fancy being around when they came. Accordingly we elected to set off for Meadow Lane Lock and safety. "Can we follow you?" they asked. "Certainly," we replied, neglecting to mention that it would be a case of the blind leading the blind, and off we went. I sat on the bows with a powerful torch to assist the searchlight, but I think we were only on half throttle for the current carried us sideways to some extent. At any rate, a red marker buoy came up to starboard, and from somewhere out in the darkness there came the dull, dangerous roar of the weir not far away. We swung to port and put more speed on. It was difficult to judge our exact position in the moonless night, with car lights ashore tending to blind and confuse us. I began to wonder if we had done the right thing. The river seemed to carry on forever with us searching vainly for some sign of Meadow Lane Lock to one side. Suddenly a light flashed onto the lock gates. Our lock keeper friend had seen us and was showing the way. We slid gratefully into the chamber and he locked us up so that he and my father could nip off for a drink before closing time. "That was hairy," the other boatowner said, "lucky you know the river". I put him wise and he walked away looking thoughtful.

We assumed that the Trent had no more experiences in store for us but in the event we were proved wrong. An easy day was spent around Meadow Lane before we departed in the late afternoon to tie up at Beeston for the night. Early morning found us locking through back onto the river and we had only gone a short distance when we realised that the current had become much swifter than before. My mother unwrapped a chocolate bar putting the paper overside and we watched it disappearing astern at high speed. Our progress ahead was slow by comparison and it became obvious that we had very little power in hand. A dredger lay in the centre of the stream so that in an emergency we could try to put a line aboard that. Alternatively, we could have reduced power and let the flow take us backwards to Beeston Lock. We had no anchor or cable aboard should the engine have failed, and I learned early on in life that it is best to carry these items aboard when dealing with a powerful river like the Trent. But our sturdy little engine did not fail. We used the bends as best we could, going around on the inside to avoid the worst, yet it was still touch and go as we slowly approached the tail of Cranfleet Weir with a torrent coming down, swirling across the cutting to the lock further on. The only way was to proceed crabwise facing this rushing stream, edging sideways towards the lock. Suddenly we were out of the current and heading straight for the bank and we had to make a swift alteration of course.

Once in the lock we were informed that navigation had been stopped on the river due to the swift current and that we should not have been allowed past Beeston. "Does it often flood like this?" we asked. "It's all the bloody rain," our informant replied mournfully. We nodded and understood. Looking for a mooring at Sawley, we came to a suitable piece of bank and my father went forward so as to leap ashore. Losing his balance he reached for the grabrail but instead picked up the boathook lying beside it. He disappeared over the side still clutching the implement in his hand. We stopped at Sawley to dry out yet again thus allowing time for the river beyond to drop.

Soon NIPPY was back in the quieter waters of the canal where we could make steady progress without any concerns over weirs or the current. The returning fleet had separated so that we were once more travelling quite on our own and it was possible in those days to travel many miles without coming across another moving boat. Reaching a lock we hardly bothered to see if anything was coming the other way since it was seldom the case. So we soaked up the leisurely miles. Stone boatyard lay basking in the sun, the covered dry docks with their charming mellowed brickwork. There was a handful of craft outside mostly belonging to one of the few hire boat companies operating at that time with a brewery just beyond. Stone was also the place where I fell in or rather jumped owing to a miscalculation. The boat had been coming alongside and I had a rope in my hand. A passing zephyr of wind blew the bows out, yet I still made a spring for the shore thinking that I could make it. A heavy splash and that cold, sodden feeling told me otherwise and it was drying out time yet again.

Nearing Stoke, we came up to Sideway Colliery where the National Coal Board were building up the subsiding banks and carrying colliery waste in their attractively painted craft. A narrow boat lay at the loading point itself. She was the SILVER JUBILEE belonging to Potter & Sons, and I can still see the name panel with its smart green background. The entire boat had a well cared for look about it, the brasswork all freshly rubbed and bright. The old captain and his wife greeted us royally as we passed then turned to load their craft as the coal began spilling off the endless belt, down a chute to the hold. The last time we had gone through Stoke Locks the flight had been devoid of traffic, but today was different. Climbing up through the locks, we came across a boat youth, roughly my own age, careering along the towpath aboard a very battered-looking bicycle, twirling a windlass nonchalantly in hand. "Look out, there's a motor boat coming," he yelled without slackening speed. We peered around the bend, not yet fully acquainted with canal parlance and expecting to see some sleek and varnished craft. Sure enough there was indeed a boat, painted in Anderton's colours with twenty tons aboard.

We noted the Caldon Canal, which joins just above Etruria Top Lock. This most attractive and interesting waterway also provides a conduit for water from Rudyard Lake, which at 170 acres is an invaluable source of water for the main line.

Onwards through Stoke we went, looking for somewhere suitable to tie up for a meal when we saw a fish and chip shop and stopped nearby. Preparing to set off again we were surprised to see SILVER JUBILEE coming through the bridgehole now laden with coal, bound for Middlewich. Her elderly crew must have wasted no time in getting the cargo aboard and setting off behind us. His name was Danny Jinks and he and his wife retired soon afterwards to their canal-side cottage in Middlewich, where they would come out to wave cheerily as we passed by. I remember that afterwards SILVER JUBILEE was taken over by someone only a little younger. We loosed off the mooring lines to follow the laden craft at a respectful distance behind. This gave us time to see the many wharves, some of which were still in use. Here we would see a place with pottery materials brought by water, or perhaps a heavy door set into a wall that was obviously in use, and then come across an actual boat being unloaded by shovel and wheelbarrow. Regrettably, there were many firms that seemed to have given up using the canal. We passed once again the boatyard now busy at work. There was a lifting gantry at one end of it as I remember, for they had the stern end of a narrow boat raised up for repair. We had lagged far behind the old couple so that when we arrived at Harecastle, they were already in, doors closed behind them and the ventilation fans turned on. Then it was our turn. Once again we found the tunnel experience rather unpleasant and were glad to reach the other end. It was now but a short distance to Hardingswood Junction, our mooring for the night. We had sat down for the evening meal when a loaded pair came through the twinned top locks. The motor boat passed us very close, its single cylinder diesel going flat out so as to get the butty boat moving. We watched in fascination as loose objects danced about in the vibration transmitted through the water.

Our homeward journey was now well advanced as we sailed along that branch of the Trent & Mersey which links it with the Macclesfield via the little stop lock at Hall Green, hidden away in a cutting with a wrought iron footbridge going to a house on the far side. They kept hens and supplied some of the best white eggs that I have ever tasted. There remained a good quantity of loose weed around the head of the lock which made us fear the worst, but we pressed on regardless hoping for the best and were pleasantly surprised for much of it had been gathered by our return, though we still had trouble in places. I remember a luxuriant variety of water lily in the area of Ramsdell Hall with its trim lawn extending to the canal edge, and it made me wonder if they had been planted for effect. We did not meet another moving craft all the way to Bosley Locks, some 9 miles from Hall Green. How different it would be today. Some of the lock ponds were low and one in particular completely dry. We ran enough water down to float NIPPY through the lowered ponds and made our way to the summit. Onward through the summit level, we noted how less well maintained it was than the Trent & Mersey. We were on an almost forgotten backwater. One tended to observe this when travelling any distance. A canal in daily commercial use tended to be much better maintained than one where it had dried up. For this reason the pleasure boaters then supported the idea of keeping working craft alive, although a subtle change came later on.

Through the pleasant miles to Marple and down the locks, we came across Chris the lock keeper, who gladly helped us on our way despite the fact that it was again raining heavily. My father had quite a nasty fall on the steep towpath as the final lock was negotiated, so we stopped a while and rested at our favourite spot, hoping for the rain to ease but it never did. The Swingbridge at Woodley had caused little trouble in the past, yet now it was an absolute brute. We sweated for ages trying to move the thing and still it would not budge. "The farmer closes it with his tractor," advised a passing fisherman. In the end we found a hefty length of timber which could be used as a lever to move the recalcitrant bridge.

We were now on the final leg of our journey as NIPPY came to the top lock at Fairfield. We had sent a message ahead for Walter, and dependable as ever, he was there not long after we arrived with one of his mates giving extra help as we locked steadily down. All went well until Clayton Lane Lock was reached, here the gates turned out to be obstructed and of course there could be no question of using the boat to clear them this time. Still they were not beaten. One gave the other a lift over a factory wall, and he was soon back with a long ladder having obviously done this before. So with the obstruction shifted and the final two locks accomplished, it only remained for NIPPY to sail up the familiar arm of canal after our absence of a month or more.

We emptied her of provisions and bedding, feeling keen regret on my part, for despite the bad weather it had been a most interesting trip that had taught me something of our inland waterways. I loved the sense of variety, for every day seemed to be different somehow. I had liked seeing the working boats about which I had heard, and pondered whether if someday I should work on the canals, should there be any still in use, since the future then was so much in doubt. No doubt however could exist about the staunchness of our boat. She had carried us safely through canal and flowing river with hardly a blemish anywhere to show for it excepting some minor scratches here and there, and I think my father was rather proud of her. We washed her down before tying on a tarpaulin, open at both ends in order to keep the rain off yet allowing air to circulate. There she remained all winter long, nestling in the reeds still populated by softly clucking water hens.

Cruising in the Fifties

Part One - To Market Drayton

As spring brings out the daffodils to flourish once again, covering the fields and grassy banks in their optimistic hue, so do the thoughts of the boating fraternity return once more in hope and anticipation towards the season to come. Those little jobs lingering through autumn and the long winter now take on a note of urgency at many a mooring and boatyard. It is often the case with boatowners and certainly was so with us.

Though satisfied in the main with the performance of our boat, the cockpit arrangement remained rather poor with some need of improvement. We had devised a homemade folding cover out of waterproofed canvas and tubular steel, which although it kept out the weather had certain disadvantages including a tendency to nip the fingers of the operator. It had to go. In its place we decided to make a small cabin open at its forward end with a centre sliding section running over it closing over the windscreen, and we had her lifted out in order to do this. What it lacked in beauty was more than made up for in practicality and the new arrangement stayed with the boat until it was rebuilt many years later. Then to the paint and varnish which we bought from our nearest chandlers C.B Cross on the corner of Deansgate, a well established firm known to many enthusiasts in the Manchester area then, and so with her surfaces freshly aglow she was ready for the water once again.

It had never been our intention to keep NIPPY on the Ashton, our idea was to use her in order to escape the city grime and seek the countryside, so accordingly we had joined the North Cheshire Cruising Club some little time before. Their headquarters were situated on an arm of canal at High Lane, towards the northern end of the Macclesfield, where we went in order to make arrangements. Regrettably, the official we met there was not very optimistic about our finding a mooring on the arm and tended to be rather unhelpful. We came away with a feeling of disappointment but in fact he turned out to be untypical of the North Cheshire. Instead we went to Marple Pool, just above the top lock and called at a rather ramshackle pavilion on the far side, headquarters of the local British Legion. We asked the caretaker about moorings along their frontage. "Certainly," he said. "Whereabouts?" we asked. "Oh, anywhere along there," he replied, indicating the nearly deserted wharf. Only two boats were present, a small cruiser BLUEBIRD and a big old centre cockpit craft called PATHAN (pronounced patahn). This latter craft had once been involved in an accident when passengers had been sunbathing on the roof as she travelled along. Coming to the low bridges at Poynton, they realised the danger a little too late and somebody lay trapped between boat and bridge. Luckily the incident did not cause a fatality, although the person concerned was crippled for life, which only goes to show that even placid canal travel can have its dangers.

This turned out to be a marvellous place to keep a boat, with fine views over the distant hills and two attractive canals on which to sail. The caretaker kept an eye on things and he told me of its history. It had once been a limekiln and the stone had come from Buxworth at the top end of the Peak Forest. After unloading, the boats could go down four locks of the Marple Flight to Posset Bridge where an arm used to go off, connecting with the kilns at lower level so that processed lime could be loaded straight aboard. Jinks' boatyard had been situated on the other side of the pool where many a narrow boat had been built and the dry dock could still be seen although it was no longer in use. Old Johnny, a retired boater, told me that the custom had been to start a new boat on the bank, then to launch her down primitive ways before completion and finish her off in dry dock, thus making way for yet another new boat and making best use of the land available. Jinks had also owned the pavilion, which he used as a dance hall. It was certainly a cheerful little place held together by enthusiasm more than anything else. They still held dances and on one occasion took up the floor for repair, to find a gaping hole underneath where once a kiln had been.

The modifications to NIPPY had taken us well into summer, but we would not have missed our annual holiday on any account. This year it was to be a much less ambitious trip to Market Drayton on the main line of the Shropshire Union since we had not the time to go further, although we looked forward to it with the same keen anticipation as before.

Accordingly, on one sunny Saturday morning we untied her and did again the flowing miles to Bosley Locks where we went down just the one to tie up overnight in what the boaters and canalmen called 'Long Pond'.

We were up early the following morning, with me all ready to be off. Although the weed along this lower level was less than in the previous year, it still gave us trouble causing a halt on many occasions to free a blocked water intake when the fine chickweed had been drawn in. We finally gained Hardingswood Junction in the late afternoon, where we now turned left and started down the first of the locks, which took the Trent & Mersey to Middlewich some twelve miles away. Many were twinned and known collectively as 'The Cheshire Locks' or more simply as 'The Cheshires'.

As we proceeded down I studied the layout carefully to note which had been the original lock with not only the towpath being an infallible guide but also in the different design of the two arches where a bridge spanned below a pair of locks. Curiously, although the Trent & Mersey was much used by heavy craft at that time, we actually went hard aground through cutting a bend a little tight. So far we had seen no traffic so I asked a lock keeper leaning on his garden gate if anything was likely to be about. He did not share my enthusiasm. "Fair brings the plaster down sometimes when they open them bolinders up," he muttered darkly.

We had tied overnight below the two single locks above Hassel Green, and it was still early morning when there came the urgent rattle of paddle gear and the heavy note of an engine. It turned out to be two motors and a butty belonging to Mersey Weavers, the Stoke-on-Trent carriers that as previously stated had absorbed Andertons, the other main carrier in that area a few years before, and their craft were an amalgamation of the two. They were loaded with gravel for Manchester, their crew struggling with the reluctant engine of the boat SPAIN. The butty drifted over towards us. "Push it away if it comes near," the boatman's wife called and came across to help, shrugging on a heavy coat against the onset of rain. "These engines are always breaking down nowadays," she said, "Can't beat the old hoss". Two plumes of smoke could be seen in the distance, and then a pair of British Waterways boats came into view, loaded with flour from Manchester to Burslem in Stoke-on-Trent. "Here's some of your mates," I said to her as they eased down, the cratch of the motor extended into a graceful bulk. "No, they're not us, them lot," she replied, glaring down at the leading steerer who smiled nervously back. Someone later said that the flour traffic had once belonged to them.

The history of this traffic is most interesting. Records show that James Hall, the Ashton carrier, had a regular agreement to take flour from a mill on the Hollinwood Branch to the Trent & Mersey. The final destination is not stated, although it may only have gone as far as Stoke, since his boat would return only a few days later, now loaded with soda ash for a firm on the Ashton main line.

On the Upper Peak Forest

We shared the locks at Middlewich

Great Haywood Junction, 1958

MALVERN near Market Drayton on the Shropshire Union, 1957

EAGLE and butty at Nantwich, 1957

Craft of the Mersey Weaver Fleet passing through the Twinned Plants Lock, Hardingwood Junction, Trent & Mersey

Seddons salt boat being loaded at Middlewich, 1957

Andertons managed to gain a foothold on this traffic for whatever reason in 1928 and then took it over entirely. Was this flour taken to the Burslem Arm?

Yet another pair could be seen coming down and now we were suddenly in the thick of it all, moored below the locks and surrounded by laden craft. My father took the only sensible way out and set off for Hassal Green where we hoped to find some shops and a little more space. We tied up there and helped the traffic boats down, not that they were in much need of assistance. The last pair turned out to be Potter & Sons' boats loaded with coal for Middlewich, their boat names always seeming to begin with the letter 'S'. The lock at Hassal Green was still twinned at that time and they made short work of passing through it, smoke from their cabin chimneys brushing silently against the ancient brickwork, then the bottom gates were opened and like the smoke itself they were gone.

We followed at a more leisurely pace since in our case there was no need to hurry. Near Booth Lane we came across a horse-drawn day boat and it was good to see it since I had thought that all such craft had left the waterways altogether. Middlewich now came into view and we stopped opposite a chip shop near to Kings Lock. The first lock up to the Middlewich Branch was infamous for having a fierce turbulence in the filling and so forewarned we treated it with the proper care. Our day ended near to Church Minshull, with views across that wasting asset, the River Weaver. The next day found us following yet another loaded pair bound this time for the Black Country, though I forget what they carried. We hung behind as they tackled Cholmondeston Lock, noting how much more troublesome for them a single lock was. They waved us past near Barbridge Junction with its warehouse spanning the cut and I noticed right away how much deeper the Shropshire Union was in that area so that we fairly surged along.

Nantwich Basin marked the end of the old wide beam Chester Canal, and was also the home of some rather splendid pleasure boats belonging to Nantwich & Border Counties Yacht Club. Their boats certainly lived up to the title and the Shroppie itself seemed more genteel than the workaday Trent & Mersey, with its rolling countryside and beautifully tailored locks. A pleasure craft was about to enter the two at Hack Green as we approached, and they paused to let us share since we were all on strict instructions from British Waterways not to waste water and to share whenever possible. Commercial traffic seemed lighter now but this was compensated for by a notable increase in pleasure craft. Sometimes there would be three of us sharing a single lock though I would not recommend it. We thought of a 35-foot cruiser as being quite large and would be duly impressed, trying to imagine all the space inside. The two craft separated above the locks and we settled back to enjoy all that was new until we reached the fifteen at Audlem.

Canal builders did not always lay out their design for the benefit of users. Canal junctions will be formed at difficult angles, balance beams sometimes project well over the lock sides, whilst at Audlem and elsewhere, the byewashes run right across the lock tail, deflecting any entering craft onto the opposite wall as the scarred brickwork testifies. We fought our way through this to find the locks themselves in good condition and very easy to operate. We stayed overnight somewhere in this vicinity.

There is another flight of five at Adderley and these were child's play after Audlem, and then it was onwards to Market Drayton where we stayed at the wharf for a day or two. There was also a lay-by to one side where British Waterways had a workshop for the making of concrete piles, some of them being taken away by boat. A hire cruiser yard had been established on the other side and it seemed to be doing well. We had a long chat with other boatowners including one who told us that he had been coming out of a lock and whilst passing the top gate had caught the projecting collar band common to this area, which had holed his craft just above the water line. We walked down to the little town once or twice, noting how fast the road traffic seemed to be going after our leisurely days on the water. Everyone seemed in indecent haste to reach their destination and I could not help wondering as to what was so urgent. We miss so much in travelling by road, horses in the paddock here or an interesting bit of architecture there, and whilst any canal destination can be reached by road, there is not the same sense of achievement as we felt, strolling around the old town.

Soon it was time to start on our homeward path, and fully provisioned again we turned the boat around to set off on a lovely sunny morning which I remember well. A laden single motor boat was approaching as we neared Adderley and the steerer signalled us to depart from the usual passing rule since the deep water was to his left. We did this and MALVERN slid past with its fully sheeted load and I noted how young the steerer was as we passed, perhaps being in his early teens.

The boat belonged to British Waterways North West Division Carrying Fleet, which subdivided into the northern fleet, being Leeds & Liverpool short boats based at Wigan, and the southern fleet at Anderton near Northwich. This second fleet consisted largely of craft formerly belonging to the carriers Fellows, Morton & Clayton. British Waterways were having some new craft built around this time. Two traditional butties had come from Walkers of Rickmansworth on the Grand Union, whilst some all-steel craft of a new design had been built by Isaac Pimblotts and by Yarwoods, both of Norwich, known as the Admiral Class with names like MOUNTBATTEN and JELLICO. They were built of thinner, high tensile steel with the aim being to carry more cargo on the same draught. Waterways had also invested in some new engines including the two cylinder air-cooled Armstrong Siddeley.

Downwards through Adderley and Audlem we went until we were brought to a halt by an unusual delay. A pair of boats had been ahead of us and as we came to Hack Green Locks it was evident that something had gone wrong. The pair were loaded with steel tubes which because of their length forced the removal of the draw chains during loading, otherwise there is a tendency for the sides to spread slightly if they are not tightened across the hold, which evidently had happened here and the butty was firmly wedged between the chamber walls. They had tried everything they knew, running water down to try and flush her out, lowering the short pond to see if this would free her but finally it was a case of shifting cargo. The captain was a young man in his early twenties and a boat youth with him I imagined to be his brother. A woman, who could well have been the mother of the two, stood in the butty hatch. They dropped down, lithe as cats, and started to loosen the heavy tubes with a short bar of wood inserted into the end of each, restacking the load until eventually the boat was free. I later described this incident to a former boater named Charlie Roberts, who said that his practice had been to load most of the tubes before tightening the draw chains back and then to place the last of the tubes on top. Apparently it was a regular cargo from the Midlands. This delay combined with the heavy locking had slowed us down so we called it a day at Nantwich Aqueduct and saw the town on the following morning.

We had noted the start of the Llangollen Canal on our outward trip, so now on our way back we decided to stop and have a look. This waterway was said to be the Mecca of canal travel and very beautiful, although somebody we knew that had been along, reported it very shallow in places, so it seemed a good idea to stop and enquire. The Llangollen begins with a flight of four locks and we hung around waiting for a boat to come down, but there was no movement save the trickling of water through the gates, the hovering of butterflies and droning of bees to disturb a warm and peaceful summers day. We had a leisurely cruise after that and it was still early when we stopped at Church Minshull.

The weather continued very fine as we did the remaining miles of the Middlewich Branch, arriving in that town just after midday. I said little to anyone, but took my camera and walked down past the narrow locks and under Town Bridge to where I knew I would find a salt works that owned a fleet of boats. Seddons works stood on the towpath side with a winding hole opposite and boats standing empty, though still sheeted up, for Seddons protected their commodity well. A projecting canopy extended from the works to cover the towpath and canal itself. This protection even went to the loading of craft as I could readily see, for they were carefully stacking the bags of salt aboard a motor boat as I arrived. The mast and stands had been packed around with straw and bound with tarpaulin, which also lined the hold. A figure stood waiting in the boat so I took his photo. Soon the others came bustling out with a simple, four wheel truck piled high with the snow-white bags. "Has he got you in that little box mate?" they asked whilst continuing to load apace. Then they were off for another load, leaving me to reflect that apart from Sideway Colliery, I personally had not seen any boat on the Trent & Mersey loaded or unloaded by anything else other than by hand. Once again they arrived with another truckload and the lean hull settled deeper in the water. There would be a cheery word for the occasional passer-by and even for myself despite the many questions. It was hard but not unpleasant work to which they were accustomed. At night they would go for a drink with their mates and they seemed to be content, and contentment is a precious thing to be savoured and enjoyed.

I moved over to the cabin where the company name had been written on a red name panel rich in decoration. I was looking at something not done for the benefit of the tourist but because Seddons liked it that way. Walking on, I went down past big lock towards the aqueduct beyond and when I returned the boat was loaded and ready for sheeting up.

In fact we were now ahead of schedule so that we had time in hand to turn downwards through Middlewich Locks and some distance beyond before returning to tackle the steep climb up to the summit. Once again, there were working craft around mostly operating in pairs. Going upwards to Stoke they would always be loaded, although sometimes were empty when returning down. Evening found us mooring at Wheelock Wharf, where forewarned we decided not to tie up at the centre of it but to one end. Sure enough, soon afterwards we were joined by commercial craft and the place suddenly became more crowded. I watched as the boaters' social life unfolded before me. After the evening meal some of the men disappeared off to the pub whilst the women busied around finding things to do, socialising on other boats or shouting instructions to the children off on some jaunt of their own. Watching this I realised that we were overlooking a scene that had not changed really all that much in a good many years, but of course we were also a part of it. "Watch yer boat when yer set off," they said. "There's a sunken wall over there," indicating to the far side. "Fair take the bottom out of `er it will". By the time we arose for breakfast they were gone.

We continued the climb up the Cheshire Locks, making leisurely progress until evening found us tying up by the now familiar junction at Hardingswood. Later on as twilight slowly turned into night, a pair of loaded Mersey Weaver boats joined us and the evening livened up considerably. They were a youngish couple and they had a little girl. It was of course bad manners to gaze into the interior of boat cabins, though we did have a glimpse of the neatness within. Many Mersey Weaver boats looked as though they wanted docking in these the final years of canal carrying, although the boaters clearly did their best to keep them as smart as they could.

It was my first opportunity to have more than a few brief words with working boaters living on the cut, though it soon became apparent that they were just as interested in us. The ice broken, they enquired about our lifestyle, where we lived, where we went on holiday and so on. In return they told us about their arduous life, how one young man had married somebody 'off the bank' but she could not stick the long hours, the heavy work or being cramped in a tiny cabin. It seemed that life had been even harder in the past, where sometimes the wives or children had no option but to walk for miles with the horse. I suppose that they could see an end to their increasingly fragile world and were finding out what the future might hold for them ashore. I wished them well, yet felt sorry at the thought of the canal losing a boating family. In fact, we were to see them again a couple of years later and they were still on the cut, working this time for British Waterways. They told us that they were used to travelling on the Trent & Mersey and did not like it if a stoppage somewhere forced them to go around via the Shropshire Union, which must have added time to their trip. They described carrying various cargoes including baled up empty sacks on the River Irwell in Manchester, which tended to make them fairly unstable so that they would rock alarmingly in the wash of other craft. Other subjects raised included the working of locks. "Why do your lot always shut all the gates?" they asked, and we explained that it was because British Waterways told us to. "Well, it makes more work for us," they said and added that they rarely did, except where they were aware that a particular lock was leaking badly. "A lock with all the gates shut is set for nobody," they said. Typically, they set off the following morning before we were up, the motor boat, which I think was called WILLIAM taking up the heavy tow. They were a decent, hard-working couple and we could only wish them well.

On returning home, I lost no time in asking Walter for his opinion regarding the shutting of gates. He considered the point carefully, "Firstly always drop the paddles after use. Never leave them up. Always close the top gate afterwards, unless of course a boat is waiting to go down. The reason for it is that bottom gates are more prone to leakage. Regarding bottom gates," and he paused for thought, "you could leave them open provided that you are quite sure that all the top paddles are down and there is no great leakage from the paddles or gates." He then taught me how to look out for water leaking past the gate paddles and boiling up in the chamber. "I like to see the bottom gates left open," he said, "because if they are closed it means that some person could fall into an empty lock and not be able to get out. The LNER never insisted on shutting them anyway".

We followed Walter's advice after that and usually left the bottom gates open after making sure that everything was shut at the top end. This would not have assisted the boaters much, however, for going uphill they could push the bottom gates open again with their boat. It was the action of shutting the top gates which must have delayed them, especially on a heavily locked section such as the Cheshire Locks. In fact British Waterways made this request because pleasure boaters were more prone to wasting water by leaving the paddles up, and the insistence that all gates be left shut tended to safeguard against this to some extent. The obvious problem of somebody not being able to get out of an empty chamber they consider to be solved by the fitting of lock ladders for such an eventuality. Whether a person could swim over to scale one of these in sopping wet clothing is open to speculation. Be that as it may, the practice of closing all gates is well entrenched and screams of rage would arise from all sides if one had the temerity to leave them open now.

Part Two - To Tixall

Our fondness for canal travel had in no way diminished as we opened the maps in order to decide on our destination for the cruise of 1958. This unique way of touring the English countryside had impressed us right from the start, with many places left to visit on a system covering 2000 miles.

We finally decided upon Braunston, a busy canal centre situated at the intersection of the Grand Union and the Oxford canals. We realised that to pass through Birmingham meant negotiating a fair number of locks, climbing up to the Birmingham level and then descending on the other side, when to go around seemed the better choice. Sailing along the Trent & Mersey to Fradley Junction and then turning right would take us there via the Coventry and the Oxford canals.

However, it was me who let the side down. I always suffered in summertime with the dreaded hayfever, which this year for some reason was severe and worsening as our journey progressed. Finally, it turned into bronchitis and I was fighting for my breath. Alarmed, my parents stopped at Great Haywood in order to call a doctor. He treated me and advised us to stay where we were so that he could call again. This put paid to any thoughts of our reaching Braunston for that year. We simply had to face the facts and save it for another time.

There can be few places more suitable for an enforced stay than Great Haywood and its environs. It was a peaceful location with a village within easy reach. There was also a bridge constructed massively of stone to take the traveller over the Trent to Shuckburgh Hall on the other side, which had to remain out of bounds for me. There were a handful of craft by the junction, the largest being a former inspection boat belonging to a family who ran a boatyard in Birmingham, Keays I think their name was. They said how easily the yard could be run, their men being of great experience knowing exactly what to do without being told. The bulk of their work would be to repair the day boats, or Joey boats as they were sometimes called, for which that complex system of waterways known as the Birmingham Canal Navigations were famous and where a vast tonnage once was moved. I still felt rather short of breath otherwise I would have asked them more than I did.

Someone told us about a place known as Tixall Wide about a mile along the Staffordshire & Worcestershire Canal and they urged us to visit, so a day or so later we did. We had expected to see something alike to Marple Pool, not the lake that opened up before our surprised gaze, its true length concealed by a curve to the left. It really was a most compelling spot and here we remained for some time.

The original NIPPY had long succumbed. It had been stolen by some youths and suffered a battering in the process before being retrieved. Now it had been broken up, its place taken by a brand new fibreglass dinghy, some eight feet in length. What it lacked in character was balanced by its durability. On one occasion, I had seen it leaned upon by an empty pair of boats, trapped between them and the unyielding bank. The sides contracted inwards and I fully expected to hear a loud splintering crack, instead of which they expanded back again and pushed the pair away.

The first NIPPY had also been a sailing boat so there was nothing else for it but her successor should be the same. I first made a fitting for the mast and then fashioned a lugsail out of Egyptian cotton bought from C. B. Cross. A long shallow keel and a rudder made her complete. There had been nowhere really to try her out apart from the restricted Marple Pool yet now as I came off the sick list again, here was an idyllic place. A soft summer breeze stole across the lake to rustle the reeds on the other side whilst in the distance the expresses ran far enough away so as not to intrude.

We would also do a leisurely cruise of perhaps a few miles before returning in the evening. Finally, we turned her round and set off back to Marple. It had been rather different from cruising many miles a day, although in a way it was just as enjoyable.

Part Three - To Stourport

The Staffordshire & Worcestershire had intrigued us in the previous year so our destination for 1959 had to be Stourport where it joined the River Severn. The first part turned out to be pleasant enough though not really outstanding. Apart from Tixall Wide it contained a section just before Autherley where the canal narrowed to little more than a boat's width for quite a long distance, widening every so often for the boaters to pass. It was the southern half that I remember more. In places it had been hewn from rock, with caves at one location carved out for dwellings in the past. There was also a high, rocky bank overhanging the canal known locally as the Austcliffe Rock. In another area it ran for miles through dense woodland, the high trees in places almost touching overhead. So we followed this ancient canal, its downward passage to the Severn speckled with the occasional lock.

The chief engineer had been James Brindley (1716 – 1772) who came from near Tunstead in the Peak District of Derbyshire. He started life working on the land before being apprenticed to one Abraham Bennet of Gurnett, then a village near Macclesfield close to where the canal now runs. He was barely literate, yet this did not prove a handicap for he was an original thinker, being able to solve many problems in his head, a rare gift indeed. The scope of a millwright was very wide and apart from designing machinery he had already done a survey for a canal from Trent to Mersey, an idea of Earl Gower and the potter Josiah Wedgwood. His work eventually brought him to the attention of Francis, the Third Duke of Bridgewater at his estate in Worsley near Manchester. The

Duke and his agent John Gilbert planned to build a canal from there to Manchester for the carriage of coal etc, which would include an aqueduct over the River Irwell, something quite new in England at that time that raised considerable doubts and scepticism.

The three combined to beat the sceptics, each bringing his own talent to the fore. The Duke had seen such aqueducts built in Europe, whilst Gilbert himself was clearly a very talented man. As for Brindley, he eventually became chief engineer for the Trent & Mersey, Coventry, Oxford, Chesterfield, Birmingham, Droitwich and Staffordshire & Worcestershire canals, of which only the latter did he live to see completed about a year before his death. All of the canals on the grand cross linking the Severn, Thames, Trent and Mersey had been surveyed and in the main engineered by him, a very fine achievement for one who started out in life working as a farmhand.

Finally, we arrived at the entrance lock to Stourport Basins and the lock keeper hurried out to work us through, advising on the best place to moor. Some of the basins had been filled in by this time, which still left a considerable area of water giving rise to speculation as to how busy this location must have been at one time. Two sets of locks connected with the Severn, one for narrow and another for wide beam craft, with a dry dock situated so as to make use of the fall. A large pub known as 'The Tontine' stood on the bank dividing the basins from the Severn. We all felt it had an intriguing air of decadence about it notably around the basins themselves. One building supported a clock tower prominently displaying the time, though appropriately the hands had ceased to move. The river looked big and inviting but we did not go further except to travel briefly on a tripping boat and to explore the town itself.

We had decided not to travel back exactly as we had come, but to make a detour along the Shropshire Union Main Line where it joins at Autherley. The weather was gloriously hot and sunny as we followed the Staffordshire & Worcestershire on its winding course, with thick layers of tar melting on the lock balance beams as we worked our way through. There is a flight of three locks at Bratch where a steep hill is climbed. They are not strictly speaking a staircase, since a few feet of water divides each lock from the next, with the lock ponds extended laterally. A mistake could easily be made here so it is advisable to study the layout carefully before lifting a paddle.

At Autherley Junction we turned left to enter the stop lock with which the Shroppie begins, known to the boaters as 'Cut End'. An office brightly bedecked with flowers was situated alongside, and somebody issued forth, which we knew could only be one Sammy Lomas. Dear old Sam. He was famous throughout the waterways for his friendliness and helpful attitude towards pleasure boaters and for being, well, a character that one had to meet. He had started as a lad checking tolls at Kings Lock Middlewich, but had arrived a day or two early. "What shall I do then?" he asked the toll collector. "Sit and watch the boats go by," he was told. "And I have been watching them ever since," said Sammy. He realised my deep interest in canals when we had a long talk. One thing that he said stayed in my mind to be recalled many years later. "There are some who work on the canals," he said, "they finish on a Friday night and the canal can breach or do what it wants until Monday morning." Very true.

We eventually parted with Sammy to start out on this line of canal built much later then the Staffordshire & Worcestershire and the difference became apparent right from the start. Sometimes it was ruler straight, hills and valleys shrugged aside as it followed a confident course, connecting with the former Chester Canal which extended to the coast. The countryside is attractively rural with sometimes a dramatic interlude where a deep cutting occurs, containing perhaps a bridge soaring high overhead. We stopped at Norbury where there is a maintenance yard opposite to a junction and a branch that at one time took the traveller to Newport and Shrewsbury. It now led only to a dry dock a little further down. The locks are all grouped in flights except for the solitary one at Wheaton Aston and are generally easy to work. Through the flight at Tyrley we passed and then found ourselves in familiar territory as Market Drayton was reached. We were back on a commercial route and it was good to see them again. Only British Waterways remained as carriers along this once busy artery, which had included cargoes of oil, carried by Thomas Claytons of Oldbury. We were to meet their craft later on in our travels over the system.

After a little stop for a day or two, we were ready to move again and the locks and miles slipped easily by. Once on the move we tended to carry on through the day with only perhaps an improvised lunch without stopping unless there was some specific reason. So we reached Middlewich to begin the climb up to the Trent & Mersey summit. Mersey Weavers had been taken over by British Waterways in the previous year, which saddened us very much since we looked forward to meeting their craft so busily at work. We had tied just above Kings Lock for our usual visit to the fish and chip shop there, when a single BW motor named MULLET passed with flour destined for Burslem. We had not expected to see it again, yet a few miles further along there was MULLET tied to a wharf with a fitters van alongside. We ourselves had stopped a little further on when once again the motor boat passed by and we were getting to know her young skipper. We passed him broken down yet again before the summit level was reached, and had visited one of the nearby pubs when the distinctive note of a bolinder engine could be heard as she arose in the lock. "Take him a couple of bottles," my father suggested, convinced that everyone was always as thirsty as him, which we did.

Our new friend was not stopping but continuing onto Harecastle and beyond. I offered to give him a hand. "Jump on," he said, and we were off as he consumed the beer gratefully. As we neared the tunnel he tried to throw her into reverse, and anyone with experience of bolinder engines will know how tricky this is to do at the best of times, since there is commonly no gearbox and the engine is direct reversing. On this occasion, it died away completely, yet there was still considerable way on the boat and we were in sight of the tunnel entrance. The old tunnel lies straight ahead with the new one curving away to the left. An old narrow boat lay across this little junction, giving an angle into the latter. "Steer it," commanded the boater, diving into the engine room. I tried, however a motor boat is not really designed for steering without power. The rudder blade is smaller than on a butty boat, and the presence of the propeller just in front of it tends to impede the smooth flow of water, but I tried. The tunnel keeper stood on the old boat, waving his arms and attempting to shoo us to one side. We caught his boat with a hefty smack, loaded down as we were. Then right afterwards the engine started.

Leaving him at the tunnel entrance, I walked back to Hardingswood, wondering if I would ever own a narrow boat of my own. I had liked the brief sensation of handling the loaded craft, which to me was boating at its best. Many of the more active canal enthusiasts then were interested not only in keeping canals open but in commercial carrying specifically with narrow boats, partly because the revival of interest centred around the narrow canals which were often seen to be most at threat.

Apart from travelling on other waterways, we tended to use NIPPY quite often for a relaxing Sunday cruise along the Macclesfield or less frequently the Upper Peak Forest and came to know various people who did the same. There was Bill Dunderdale, who owned a boat named FINGAL. She had a steam engine for propulsion, burning waste engine oil if I remember rightly, and often to be seen on the move. Another craft had no cabinwork, being just an open launch in which the couple sat with a tarpaulin around, and they were not exactly young. As evening approached they would stop at a suitable spot so that a tent could be pitched on the bank. Another was a converted ship's lifeboat in which her owner had crossed the channel to sail the continental waterways, although of course anyone attempting this needs to possess both seagoing experience and a seaworthy craft. All of this goes to prove what a hardy and a resourceful group the pleasure boaters were and I hope this is still the case.

Part Four - To Braunston

The fact that we had not been able to reach Braunston on our curtailed cruise of 1958 still haunted us such that we had to try again, and so our destination for 1960 simply had to be that important spot on the network. We set off in determined fashion to sail across familiar territory and it was not until Fradley Junction was reached that we started to explore. This was the Coventry Canal or rather its northern end since a section of the Birmingham & Fazeley divides it into two. The canal was in a rather poor state as I recall, with an urgent need of dredging, noticeable even for us in our little craft.

For most of the trip our journey had passed through that gentle countryside of which England is justifiably proud. Now as we neared the Warwickshire coalfield, the landscape around became gradually more urban. The two locks at Galscote were eventually passed, each one taking an age to fill. Then we saw some narrow boats waiting to load at Pooley Hall, painted in the Waterway's blue and yellow. A group of boat children were skylarking around, pausing to stop and wave as we passed. There is a flight of eleven at Atherstone the first we had seen with sideponds that actually worked. The last boat had been downhill which meant that these were all full. Therefore upon closing the bottom gates one has to empty the sidepond first which half fills the lock. The sidepond paddle is then dropped as equilibrium is reached and the lock is filled in the usual way. There was at that time an appreciable traffic in coal down the Grand Union carried by British Waterways, Samuel Barlows and Willow Wren, all of whose boats we saw on the move as different loading points were passed. The junction between the Coventry and Oxford canals is really a U-turn, easily done by us yet needing sure judgement on the part of working boat crews. We pivoted round this junction, known to everyone as Sutton Stop where a Stop Lock gave access to the Oxford Canal, and where also a great fleet of craft met our gaze. They were all standing empty, awaiting orders to load, presenting a sight that I shall never forget. It was really like a floating village with boats lining both sides of the cut. Ever changing as craft were given loading orders, their places taken by the arrival of more. I gathered that at one time they could be sure of picking up a return traffic from London to Birmingham, yet this was tending to disappear so they often travelled empty back.

As originally built the Oxford had meandered around on its course as the early waterways usually did. Some straightening had been done in later years, though it was still possible to see where these original sections led off. Fine iron spans carried the towpath over each, which could also be seen at Braunston Junction where the watery highway to Birmingham went off to our right.

Samuel Barlow's yard lay a little further on with quite a number of craft laid up and for sale at various prices, one boat that I remember being the freshly docked HOOD. I spoke to the manager there about canal carrying in general in which he took a very gloomy view indeed, saying that his fleet was not worth the upkeep and that he would rather cut them up and use the boat bottoms in order to prevent coalyard stocks from settling into the ground. I have to say that in travelling around the canal system I sometimes spoke to the men who either used or organised canal transport and they often took a similar pessimistic and critical view of transport by water in general, and not purely on the narrow canals. It was such a contrast to the attitude of the boaters themselves, who for the most part were struggling to preserve the way of life that was important to them, if not to anyone else.

In the event, Barlow's official was proved to be wrong as to the value of his craft. Somebody I knew bought a steel boat from them around this time for less than four hundred pounds yet sold it again some years later for many times that sum, because in the meantime the interest in canals had grown to such an extent that a working narrow boat had become a collector's item.

Canal transport was clearly receding fast with most of it going onto the roads, which also severely affected the railways. One drawback was that both rail and water were expected, in theory anyway, to pay for the track that they used, which never applied to the road. Their track has always been looked upon as a public utility. If road haulage was expected to pay a realistic share for building and maintaining the miles of motorway and lesser roads, then it would cease to be economic overnight. A fresh enthusiasm for water transport is unfolding at the time of writing yet it does not seem to be going far enough. We need to see not merely a level playing field, but one tilted positively in favour of water transport on the larger canals and rivers where the greatest return in tonnage carried is to be found.

Worries about the narrow canal system being flooded with freight, on top of the nowadays considerable pleasure boat traffic, are quite unfounded. This cannot happen for reasons that become obvious with a little thought, apart from when exceptional conditions create what has been termed a 'niche market', the operation of narrow boats with their low capacity would be viable.

Travelling on my narrow boat over the system for the last few years, I have spoken to people on the towpath as one does, and one question frequently asked is, "When are they going to use the canals again?" meaning for commercial use. So it is clear that sending traffic by water would make sense to the general public. However, we must leave a subject that is a favourite one of mine and return to our cruise.

Barlows were an old fashioned company as could be told by a visit to their yard. Another, much newer, carrier was based just below Braunston Bottom Lock. This was the Willow Wren Canal Carrying Company formed by an enthusiast Captain Bulkely-Johnson in a brave attempt to reverse the gradual drift to road transport. Their craft were all named after birds, AVOCET, DABCHICK etc with the name panel painted green, bearing a large roundel depicting a Willow Wren.

We had rather a bad experience with a pair of these on our homeward journey. Normally the boaters would ease down as they went by so as not to cause a wash, which could be considerable. Yet early one morning, just after dawn, a pair came past us without slowing down, pulling one of our mooring pins right out with the surge. As we scrambled ashore in pyjamas I was gratified to note that the motor boat steerer lost control for some reason and they piled up on the bank about a hundred yards past. "Those two never slow down for anyone, ever," commented a fisherman on the bank. Gradually we made our way home, arranging it such that we stayed overnight at the picturesque Fradley Junction where an attractive pub 'The Swan' is situated on the canal side.

There had been developments during the years that we had been cruising. A musical called 'The Water Gypsies' written by Vivian Ellis and A. P. Herbert, starring Dora Bryan in the part of Lily, appeared on stage following a book by the latter. It toured the provinces first before going to the West End. Some of the music I thought very good and in the closing scene, the stern end of a narrow boat was seen to move off.

Following the unpopular Board of Survey Report the Government had commissioned an independent report named after its chairman Sir Leslie Bowes. This had been published in 1958 and gave an optimistic view more in line with the wishes of the enthusiasts, although of course it could only make recommendations with Parliament having the final say. Despite this, British Waterways still wished to close a considerable mileage that to them had no future. This policy became ever more clear as events unfolded. A large warehouse had been pulled down in Macclesfield and the overspill weirs on the summit level were lowered by a few inches due to excessive leakage through the banks, which made navigation even more difficult on this shallow waterway. In fact the original level can still be seen as the top of the weir at Bosley Summit Lock. The topmost locks on

Marple Flight are fairly close together with the ponds extended laterally to provide enough water. A plan to fill these in so as to provide housing was discovered and stopped in time, or otherwise the flight would have become unnavigable.

Meanwhile, I had started work for the same firm that employed my father. They were a major user of industrial water but were disgusted at the state of the canal adjacent to their works, the intake often obstructed by weeds. "They seem not to care whether we use their canal or not," remarked an engineer, Jim Roby sadly. An enthusiast himself he kept a boat on the Macclesfield canal.

I came to know another canalman, John Sandeford who would keep me informed of developments on the Ashton when we met occasionally. He told me that members of senior management from Liverpool had attempted to sail through aboard the motor boat JOEL. However, something had delayed them, presumably obstructed lock gates, so that the remainder of the inspection had to be done on foot.

A faint trickle of craft still attempted to journey through with varying degrees of success, so in order to be of help we volunteered our services to the North West IWA. Sometimes the news of a boat would come through the grapevine and we would go to assist, joining the local canal staff to help her on her way. One such was the HEATHER BELL, a motor boat belonging to the Wyvern Shipping Company. She had been hired out as camping boat. They were lucky, and sailed through in one evening from Fairfield Summit to Mill Street Lock. Unfortunately, a stoppage on the Rochdale caused them to turn back.

John Parkinson, a noted enthusiast from Southport made a more successful attempt. Also notable were two enthusiasts from the south, they were John Trueman and the Reverend Stanley Evans. Their first attempt at passing through with a hire cruiser had been thwarted due to problems with the locks. Undeterred, they tried again in the summer of 1960 and wrote to us beforehand. This time they had hired a boat, WEE McGREGOR from Maclan Cruises of Macclesfield. We met them at Audenshaw and they were full of determination, there would be no turning back this time and so it proved to be. We assisted them to Mill Street Lock from where the canal staff took over and a successful passage was made.

Meanwhile, relations between British Waterways and the IWA had fallen to an all time low. A fleet of narrow boats had been sunk in Harefield Flash on the Grand Union by British Waterways, although this was denied when challenged by the IWA. The whole affair reached the national press and the gulf between them and British Waterways became all too apparent. "Our social organisation is not constituted to deal with flat untruths in high places," wrote Aickman. The state of the Ashton had become an issue of major importance to him. He saw it as being valuable due to the amount of industry on its banks from where he felt that freight could be generated. The canal had been run down by its former railway owners, yet still made a profit from the sale of industrial water. 'If such a waterway as this is lost, we might as well go out of business' he wrote and I suppose that from British Waterway's point of view it was a chance too good to miss. Sometime afterwards I saw Johnny Sandeford and he told me that the situation was becoming desperate. "They've told us not to do any more repair work on the locks," he said all upset, "no clearance or maintenance work either". I was shocked at this for it would of course mean the end of the canal and that British Waterways intended to close it.

Everyone knew that something was about to happen. British Waterways were determined to shut the canal down with the enthusiasts just as determined to oppose, and as 1960 came to an end, a faint whiff of gunpowder lay in the air.

The Ashton Campaign

Early in 1961, British Transport Waterways began to overstamp pleasure craft licences with the words 'not valid for the Ashton Canal', but when our own licence landed on the doormat it was innocent of any stamp. Our intention was to take NIPPY back down to Clayton in order to carry out a refit although there was a campaign element in it also.

A week or two before the trip, we walked the towpath from Clayton to Dukinfield in order to see for ourselves what conditions were like – and they were very bad. Several gates were badly fouled with Lock 13 having a section of gate planking missing, whilst elsewhere there were many gaps where planking had dried out such that the seams had opened up. In addition, there was the most part of a balance beam missing, or balance pole as it was sometimes termed on the Ashton. We decided on our plans and wrote to British Waterways telling them of our intention.

We made two sill rakes for the purpose and also obtained a heavy length of tubing, with two clips to fasten this onto the stump of the missing balance pole. The dinghy was filled with assorted planking to nail over the gappy gates, and with the addition of a few other items we were ready and prepared.

Early one Saturday morning in mid-February we left the moorings at Marple to begin our journey home. Despite the early hour Jack Scarlett, the Section Inspector, stood waiting for us. Although we knew him slightly, Jack was in his official capacity today. He peered carefully at our licence in the still uncertain light. "You won't get through," he said eventually. "There's a bridge completely blocked in Dukinfield." We thanked him and carried on and he made no attempt to prevent us, for we had paid our licence fee which in those days gave us a right of way. The top gate bore a multitude of notices all intended to dissuade the intrepid navigator, including one which stated that headroom on the Ashton was restricted to only five feet.

This much-photographed notice existed for some time and attracted a good deal of speculation, so perhaps we should deal with it here. There were in fact two subsidence areas at Audenshaw and Beswick. The Audenshaw one had stopped moving to all intents and purposes some years before, although there was still some movement at Bradford and Beswick. The long level known as 'Quakers Pond' between Ancoats Top Lock and Beswick had been affected so that the ground level at the Beswick end had dropped over a period of time, and there was a low bridge. To cater for this the planking of the Ancoats Top Gate had been reduced so as to lower the water level where the canal now weired over. This was done not so much to preserve headroom under the bridge, but to prevent the canal overflowing the banks at Beswick. Sizeable craft had continued to navigate whilst in addition I often walked the towpath and never knew of a bridge so severely restricted as five feet. A survey conducted by the IWA in which I took part was carried out through the full length of the canal some time later, one aim being to establish beyond doubt the available headroom of which the lowest we found measured more than six feet. Was the notice a genuine error of administration or could it have been a spot of gamesmanship? I simply establish the facts and leave the reader to decide.

Downwards we went in fine style, with me setting the locks ahead, lifting the ground and dandy paddles, enjoying the sudden surge of water as every lock was filled. We came to Posset Bridge which carries the main Stockport Road, and underneath it the main arch for the canal. There is the horse tunnel and a narrow winding passage, dank and dark with stone steps, and very little used. I remembered a conversation some time before with old Johnny the boater, a local character who told me that he had taken his first lady love to this unlikely place for some stolen moments of passion. There must have been a festival on at the time, since according to Johnny the Marple Band were stood playing overhead. "How romantic," I had murmured, stuck for a better word. "Depends on what they were playing!" muttered an eavesdropper in the background.

The canal had been quite busy hereabouts, with Black Wharf to the right of the bend below, also an arm on the left going to the former Hollins Mill where many a boat load had been consigned. Further still we travelled coming to Lock 10, also known as Iron Rail Lock, with a warehouse just below known as The Fly Boat Warehouse. In later years both this and the wharf were occupied by Vesseys, builders merchants who also used the canal. A boater sometimes employed by them was one Jimmy Bradley, who later worked for the famous carriers Fellows, Morton and Clayton. He had a bad accident, which occurred in a tunnel where he was trapped between his boat and the

Moravian Bridge

The hazards of boating

NIPPY moored on the Clayton Arm of the Ashton Canal, Spring 1961
(since filled in)

NIPPY above lock 3, Ancoats. Canal level affected by subsidence.

The official attitude in 1961, Ancoats

The Rochdale Canalmen at Castlefield Bottom Lock

Scene at Trafford Power Station, Bridgewater Canal

tunnel wall. He was eventually employed by British Waterways and, when I came to know him, lived in a house by the Anderton Lift, that miracle of engineering that connects the River Weaver with the Trent & Mersey Canal.

We negotiated the flight in around two hours with no trouble that I recall and were on our way down the Lower Peak. Onwards to Dukinfield where sure enough there was the shallow bridge that our inspector friend had mentioned, and he did not exaggerate. The bridgehole was nearly full of bricks thrown in by somebody, leaving only a narrow channel down the centre for the keel of our boat. There was nothing else for it but to put the waders on and get in, hauling the bricks out so as to improve the channel. We stacked some on the foredeck in order to lessen our draught at the after end, since with her heavy greenheart keel NIPPY tended to draw a little more than she should. After a couple of hours we had made a serviceable channel so that she could be eased cautiously through, bumping slightly over the bottom and the way ahead was then clear to Ashton Junction.

It was soon after rounding this and starting along the Ashton itself that we heard a harsh grating sound followed by a heavy bang, and the engine stopped dead. We had collided with some large underwater obstruction, a warning of things to come. We restarted the engine, but as soon as it was put into gear there came a heavy vibration noticeable throughout the boat, then we realised that some damage had been taken, probably a bent tailshaft. Keeping the revs to a minimum we crawled along as day gradually gave way to night. A tangy sweetness filled the air and told us that the premises of Robertsons, manufacturers of fine marmalade, were close at hand.

Finally we reached Fairfield Junction, our destination for the night, as indeed it must have been for many thousands who had gone before, passing through the top lock to tie by a fine stone arch which spanned the canal at its fullest width.

This was known locally as Moravian or less frequently Jamaica Bridge. The first could be easily explained since there is a Moravian settlement not far away, but Jamaica? The story as told to me runs as follows. At one time, in addition to the more mundane cargoes, casks of Jamaican rum in undiluted form were taken through, and temptation to pilfer the contents proved to be too strong. A way was found in which one of the hoops would be tapped loose so that two holes could be bored at the top and bottom, one for a drain and the other as a vent. After the required amount had been drawn the holes would be plugged and the hoop knocked home after making up the loss, hopefully not with canal water. One day they overdid it and the boat failed to turn up at its destination. A search was instigated and she was found right across the canal under the aforesaid bridge, with everyone legless apart from the horse.

The wharf to which we had tied was the base for another Fairfield carrier in former times though on a much smaller scale than that of James Hall, he had also been a Section Inspector at Marple. A substantial boathouse at one end had been built for the local inspection boat, which was now long since gone.

We spent a rather uneasy night thinking of the struggle to come, and breakfasted early. Just as we were about to depart somebody appeared through the dense early mist. It was John Sandeford. "Can't stop," he said urgently, "there's supervision about". We showed him all the equipment that we carried but he shook his head. "You won't get through," he said, "it's bad down there," though he loaned us a sill rake better than our own, and was gone. This in itself shows where the sympathies of local canalmen lay, and it was most definitely not with British Waterways. We departed with the mist still clinging around and towing her because there could be other underwater obstructions and it seemed the safest thing to do. Lock 17 negotiated, we turned the swing bridge at Copperas Lane to put her in the bridgehole where she rolled up on a drum, lifting her after end by some inches. As we struggled to get her off, a motorist loomed out of the mist before stopping abruptly, amazed at seeing a boat. A new lifting bridge had been put in at Buxton Lane some time before to which we had objected, since no mechanism had been provided at the same time in order to lift it. Now it could be moved, although with difficulty.

Approaching Edge Lane Lock we swung her out wide to negotiate British Waterways chicane, a car in the canal on one side and then soon afterwards a sunken boat on the other. Whilst we were in the lock, the supervision that we had been warned about duly appeared. Once again the licence was carefully scrutinised, but no fault could be found. "There's a balance pole missing at the next but one lock," he said. "Then you can replace it for our return trip," my father replied, with a beguiling sweetness that barely disguised what he really thought. The man disappeared soon afterwards.

Coming to Lock 14, we coachscrewed two clips to the remaining stump and fitted the tubing. I should perhaps mention here that the term balance beam or balance pole is somewhat misleading since it does not actually balance the gate as the term implies, although it undoubtedly helps. Thus a missing one is really not so catastrophic as it sounds, and by bolting a steel tube on it as a lever, we were able to move the gate. Much greater trouble lay in the fact that the bottom gates were fouled with debris which meant that we had to unload the dinghy and carry it round in order to free them. We spent some time in doing this before coming to the really bad one at Crabtree Lane.

Unusually, a swing bridge crossed right over the centre of the lock with the deepest water being at the tail end. The trick was to open the bottom paddles slowly and then thread her under the bridge as soon as ever we could. Also, there was a big hole to be repaired in the bottom gate planking. First of all we had to free the gates, a pair like which I have never come across quite so badly fouled. They were almost immovable in the half open, half closed position with debris on both sides, and it was a case of using a sill rake off the dinghy for hours in order to free them. It was mostly stone setts off the locksides along with a mass of bricks that we had to deal with until finally the gates would mitre. We never succeeded in getting them fully open, but there was a trick that we knew in order to overcome this problem. As the lock slowly filled, I worked from the dinghy nailing timber over any gaps that I found, and there were many owing to the gates being very dry with the planking joints opening wide, also there was a big hole to repair as noted in our survey.

In the midst of all this a smartly dressed figure in yachting blazer and flannels suddenly turned up, brightening the lockside and surroundings considerably. It turned out to be an official of the North Cheshire Cruising Club, who had come to see how we were doing although I have no idea how they knew about our trip since we had not mentioned it. We were very pleased to see him though, and only slightly put out when later reporting in their journal he claimed to have supervised operations.

We manoeuvred NIPPY into the lock, noting with satisfaction that the gate repairs were holding well before locking down and preparing to get her out. We pushed one gate open as far as it would go, thrusting hard upon the balance pole until an outward curve was achieved before propping it open and doing likewise to the other. The gates themselves were very old, like many on the Ashton, so it was not in fact difficult to spring them in this way, and with NIPPY being at her widest well above the waterline it made all the difference. Once through, the props could be removed and the gates resumed their normal shape.

The gates at Lock 12 were also fouled although nothing like as bad. During operations here we fished out a five-gallon drum containing bricks. “I threw that in,” claimed one youth in a burst of enthusiasm, and then hurriedly decamped. We had plenty of time in which to study the condition of these gates, which were likewise very old, and I felt concerned to see a long diagonal split in one of the mitre posts not noticed in our survey. Darkness was approaching fast as we locked through, and it became clear we would not reach our destination that night.

My father had to be at work early the following morning, it being a Monday, so I stayed overnight to watch the boat in this rather hostile place, which it still is if not even more so.

Dawn found me hard at work yet again, clearing Lock 11 and my parents turned up as I worked. I had become expert at this, fishing out one obstruction after another, which once again turned out to be the lockside surfacing, ripped up and cast into the chamber. So we came to Flannigans Lock Number 10, which had some really old gates and of course it had to be the deepest on the canal. There was rot in the heelpost of the towpath side gate where the collar band was met which caused it to lean slightly inward. Again, there were many obstructions including a sheet of corrugated iron and the remains of a wheelbarrow. I saw that a patch had been inserted in the towpath gate planking above the paddle hole. In fact the planking of older gates tends to wear at this point owing to the turbulence of water as the lock is emptied. In this case, the patch itself looked a good enough job although the gate framing that it was fixed to, seemed rather dubious. A heavy horizontal strut had been secured across the middle of this patch. We started to fill the lock and water poured out of every joint, since we had run out of timber to seal the gaps. Very slowly the level crept up for there was a considerable wastage at the gates whilst a boil of water indicated that something was amiss down below near the sill. Finally with the lock not quite full the level stopped rising, for it was in equilibrium with as much running out of the lock as coming in, and every paddle lifted at the top end that would work.

We tried forcing the top gate open against this head but it was too much. The local kids were like ants milling around and some tried to help us but it was no use. Apparently, we were beaten. Just then a workman peered over a lowish factory wall on the offside, drawn no doubt by all the commotion. He saw the predicament that we were in, bless him. "Come on lads!" he shouted to his mates. Several of them climbed over the wall and helped us to force the gate open and we were able to put the boat in.

This final head must have proved too much for the patch as it gave way at its upper part. On examination afterwards the timber above had failed so that the patch was pushed forward with the strut until it had bit into more solid timber. The effect of all this was to create a chute from which the water soared upwards and outwards in an effortless arc, slightly to one side and crashing mightily back on the bank near the byewash. The top gate closed to and the lock level dropped rapidly without the need of a paddle. We all grabbed the bow rope to prevent her from colliding with the bottom gates and I scrambled aboard as the lock emptied. Once below the level of the patch, it was possible to look right down the canal with the gates still shut. These had fouled again to a certain extent but finally we were out and clear of Lock 10 with a great sigh of relief. Looking back as we towed NIPPY along, the depth of it seemed really enormous, easily as deep as those at Marple. One account claims this to be the deepest narrow lock on the system rather than the better known one at Tardebigge. I for one would most certainly not quibble with this assessment!

No other trouble was found, so that evening saw us slipping gratefully into the Clayton Arm feeling battered and weary. Surprisingly, our boat showed little sign of her ordeal above water but we soon made arrangements to lift her out. The works crane could not be placed alongside due to a shelving bank, so NIPPY was taken a day or so later to the spot where she had been launched. She was lifted out there and a tractor and a trailer brought her back behind the house. The propeller shaft proved indeed to be bent whilst in addition a long score mark underneath was evidence that we had met with something substantial at Ashton Junction. It was fortunate that we had sheathed her in fibreglass some time before. We ordered a new shaft from Stuart Turners, and then carried on with doing a few jobs before preparing and painting the topsides and cabinwork.

The official from the North Cheshire came to see us, making sure that we had arrived safely. Soon afterwards a number of things happened in quick succession. News came of an intended cruise organised by the IWA, with the object of drawing attention to the wretched state of the canal and that somebody wanted to use it. A fleet of pleasure craft were to be gathered for the purpose to be sailed down over Whitsun. A letter was sent to the IWA referring to our recent adventure, mentioning all the gate repairs required in order to pass a fleet of craft. No reply was ever received despite the serious aspect of the matter, which made us wonder if they had got our letter, until being told sometime later by one of their council that they had received it and debated long over what to do.

It was around this time that matters took on a much more threatening note. A letter arrived from the second-in-command to a senior British Waterway's official regarding our recent trip and condemning it outright. He said that a serious wastage of water had taken place on the way down, that the locks were in a dangerous state and that any attempt to return by the same means could well have dire consequences for us with the possibility of prosecution. He finished by urging strongly that the boat should return to Marple by road. In fact we had twice asked for assistance on the Monday from their Gorton yard, yet nobody ever appeared because of course they wanted us to turn back. To my mind it was like neglecting to maintain a railway line and then blaming the engine driver and passengers when a train fell off the track. A strongly worded letter was sent by return, pointing out the work done in order to make the gates a little more watertight, which was their responsibility in any case, not ours. We did not agree to go back by road.

During this time I kept a close eye open as to what was happening along the canal, and just before Whitsun carpenters from Gorton and Wigan replaced the blown patch at Lock 10, strengthened the mitre post at Lock 12 and did other work all of which I had written to the IWA about. Finally a group from the North Cheshire 'unpaved the way', as their journal put it, by clearing bridge number 3 at Dukinfield of all the bricks, so all was ready for the Whitsun cruise.

We were truly devastated by what happened next. The evening paper carried front-page news that the bottom gates of a lock in Clayton had been destroyed by fire, and the cruise could not go ahead. Aickman was furious and described it as 'the most historically timely conflagration since the Reichstag blazed'. In view of all this, we were later most surprised to see water moving in the arm indicating that the locks were in use. A canoe came exploring up and having seen our boat ashore went quickly back. Something was clearly happening and in going up to the junction bridge I saw that a small cruiser had just gone past, bowhauled by a number of people. They knew we were there but obviously did not need our help. As soon as I could I went to see the damaged gates, which turned out to be Lock 11, just above the junction with the Stockport branch. The bottom gates had indeed been destroyed by fire and were in the chamber. How could such a thing have happened, and more importantly, who had done it? All the gates in the flight were dry owing to little use over a very long period. They were frame gates of oak construction which is normal, however the balance poles may well have been of pitch pine as favoured at one time in the area, which burns fiercely when lit. The IWA speculated as to how the gates could have finished up in the chamber, but this could have been caused simply by the fire burning through the top of the heelposts, or maybe the firemen themselves could have toppled the gates, or what was left of them into the water since they were no longer of use.

Taking the situation in, I thought that whoever had done this must have studied the area first before deciding on this particular lock. There was a factory wall to one side and a derelict lock cottage stood close by on the other, all of which would hide the wrongdoer from view to a certain extent. Also there were several avenues of escape, up or down the canal, along the Stockport Branch, or across some waste ground. Timbers of lock gates would obviously take some firing and the fire raiser would have needed much more than a box of matches. The more I thought about it the less likely it seemed to be the work of local youths. They threw bricks and rubbish in and caused general mayhem, but this was a cold calculated act clearly intended to stop the cruise taking place and somehow it did not appear to be their style.

If I remember rightly, a fire raiser or arsonist was active in the Manchester area at that time, one of those people who go around causing many thousands of pounds worth of damage and putting the lives of firemen at risk. A horrific crime somewhat rare at that time yet rather more common now. His attention could well have been drawn by the advance publicity about the cruise. Another fire occurred in September, this time destroying the bottom gates of Lock 17 where there is housing property close by. Our arsonist was becoming more bold, though I have a notion that he was eventually caught for committing similar crimes elsewhere.

Soon after the fire at number 11, I met Johnny Sandeford and he said very firmly that the fire had nothing to do with British Waterways and I believed him. He told me that senior management came to the Gorton Depot soon afterwards and they were then taken to see the damage.

The main body of the cruise had reached Fairfield and understandably turned back on receiving the news, all except for one boat. She was BRUCE, a 17-foot fibreglass cruiser from the Midlands. They set off down accompanied by a party which included council members of the IWA and a local enthusiast Fred Kemp who later told me what happened. They must have had a somewhat easier time of it than us, for much depended on how recently a boat had gone before, especially through Clayton. Local British Waterway's officials also tagged along, not so much to assist but to reiterate that the craft could not possibly use Lock 11. These same officials were taken aback when upon reaching the stricken lock everything possible was taken out of BRUCE before bodily dragging her out of the cut in order to carry her round. It was a remarkable thing to do.

The whole event was accomplished by a great wave of publicity which came, passed on by and went, leaving the canal quiet again and leaving us to fend for ourselves. There could be no question of NIPPY being carried around anywhere since she was far too heavily built; yet the instruction that she should return by road could not even be considered. It would be like slinking off with our tail between our legs. No, there remained only one answer. She must be launched again, whatever British Waterways thought, to go downwards through Manchester and onwards via the Rochdale to the Bridgewater where a great rally would be held marking the bicentenary of its opening. We had to be there. Therefore I walked the towpath again to see what the locks were like, and I found them rather better through Beswick and Ancoats. Only one pair of gates looked very old and they were at Lock No. 1. We could not delay for too long in case some other mysterious fire occurred boxing us in without hope; even so it was July before we were ready.

We launched the boat before telling British Waterways of our latest plan not long before we sailed. The young man that we had seen in the canoe came to see us and asked if we needed any help, which we did since the earlier journey had been very hard work, especially for me. His name was Keith Norgrove. This time we carried a heavy wagon sheet borrowed from the traffic department, the idea being to drape it down the front of any leaky gates so as to reduce the escape of water.

We started off on a fine Sunday summer's morning, leaving the arm for the last time as it turned out, rounding the junction onto Acid Pond. Walter was still abed as we descended through Lock 7 at Mill Street, where just beyond an arm had once ventured to Bradford Colliery. Everything went very well until we came to Lock 4 in Beswick, which although apparently shallow, is deep below the lower level due to subsidence movement, and the bottom gates would not quite mitre. Also the top gate hung open and was useless. In order to pass through we had to rake the gates so as they would close before filling not only the lock itself, but the short pond above it. We had done all of this when an engineer arrived from British Waterways, accompanied by the Section Inspector for Manchester, and without preamble brusquely demanded that we rack the paddles and gates after use. I should explain that racking the paddles etc means simply to shovel earth off the towpath into the water just above in the hope that the draw of water will seal it. Of course this is only necessary where there is much leakage and naturally it all falls out again when the lock is next filled. However, the practice could often be found on little-used and semi-derelict canals such as this one, although I once saw it done on the Trent & Mersey. The same method is used in the sealing of stop planks. His attitude caused our hackles to rise and we told him that it was not our job. The instructions to boaters said nothing about racking paddles or gates and we told him to do it himself, so there was a row. Both sides said exactly what they thought of the other, yet remarkably it cleared the air. Even so the gulf that lay between enthusiasts and British Waterways was never more obvious than at this time.

We were now in Quakers Pond, which was clear of any weed, and could motor along freely to the top of Ancoats. The reduced level here meant that there was not the usual clearance over the sill, but we made it and found ourselves gliding along behind Ancoats Hospital, the scene of altercations in the past. Some years before the Gorton Yard had received an irate letter from the hospital, asking if they could instruct their lock keeper to moderate his language when addressing boaters and towpath miscreants since it was shocking the more delicate patients, and staff were fed up with having to close the windows every time.

Yet another branch, the Islington, led away to our right. A bridge across the entrance incorporated a house at that time which made the headroom very low. A boater once told me that on one occasion they had to deliver sand to a wharf on the branch using a high-sided Bridgewater narrow boat. They realised that once empty she would not go under the bridge and so left some of the cargo in the back end of the hold, waited until nightfall and then departed.

And so to the final lock, which as already mentioned had gates that were a little ripe. A heavy piece of iron called the bumper plate hung away from the top of one, its purpose having been to protect the gate when laden craft nosed up to it going downhill. Now it was held on only by a couple of corroded bolts, so we threaded some line through the top bolt holes in order to lend support, and whilst the lock was full got away with it. Yet as the lock emptied, Isaac Newton crept back into the scene, our rope parted and the heavy plate plummeted into the lock with a great splash. My heart was in my mouth as we swung the gate for an obstruction of that size and weight would have taken some moving. Luckily the gate was not fouled.

Now we were finished with the Ashton locks and paddling along through thick weed, for there was no towpath then but arms of canal and the remains of buildings, a sign of high activity in the past. This made me think of a favourite uncle who, as a young man, carried out the menial yet necessary task of unloading the coal boats somewhere in this vicinity.

Ancoats had been a quiet area during the sixties, but at one time dire poverty stalked abroad in this place with all the consequences that follow in its wake. There was an Irish contingent with Italians living in the same district and trouble could sometimes flare between the two.

We were in flippant mood as NIPPY passed under Ducie Street where the canal was bridged by a warehouse housing many Manchester pigeons. They all took off as we passed underneath and the air was filled with the beating of wings. I knocked at the door of the Rochdale Canal Company house. It opened the merest fraction and a nose appeared around the edge, whether it was a male or female nose I never did find out. “What do you want?” it said. I explained that we wished to sail down their canal. “Come back tomorrow,” was the reply, “and in the meantime don’t tie up here, go back up the Ashton,” and the door was quickly shut. Go back up the Ashton! So we turned around to tie up to a cobbled wharf just through the bridge on the left hand side with a warehouse close by, and after a while said goodbye to our new friend who helped us so much.

A lovely day now gave way to a glorious red sunset, promising fine weather again for tomorrow. It reflected off the weathered brickwork of the surrounding buildings, redolent of great industry in the past, but now taking its ease, and it seemed that nothing could disturb this scene of utter peace.

"Tha' can't stop theer!" A powerful torch surged out from the opposite bank, a cloth-capped silhouette could be seen and it repeated the statement in watchman-like tones. We explained that until the Rochdale opened on the following morning we were unable to go anywhere, for it was the only decent mooring in the vicinity apart from above the first lock on the Rochdale, from which we had been banned for some inexplicable reason. "Well tha' can't stop theer," he said yet again, "them's bonded warehouses. I shall send for the police." The wharf was separated from the street by a pair of high, heavy gates surmounted with a fearsome row of rusty iron spikes, and sure enough soon afterwards there came a scrambling of boots and a policeman appeared over the top, dropping down on our side with the consummate grace of a sack of coal, accompanied by a crisp rending sound. He strode purposefully towards us and we were invited to inspect a small but noticeable tear in the official trousers caused by the aforesaid spikes. My heart sank at this since we seemed to be heading for a night in the cells. Luckily the light of common sense came into the proceedings for he had seen our boat at its mooring several times, and even if we had been there with felonious intent, it would surely have been the slowest getaway in history. He understood the position perfectly when we explained and bade us goodnight, going back the way he had come and I hoped that his trousers did not suffer further distress for he was a good sort.

On the following morning, we awoke to the sound of rain beating steadily down with an intensity that belied completely the promising sunset of the previous evening. Raining or not, we had locks to do, and besides it was a red-letter day. So after breakfast, we sailed her off the Ashton and onto the Rochdale, and NIPPY became the last boat to use the former physically and as a whole without being portaged around any lock since the canal had been opened for traffic in the 1790's. This seemed appropriate somehow, for she was built not far from the banks of the waterway and owned by people with long associations to the area. And so a little piece of history was made on that day, the 10th July 1961.

We presented ourselves at the Rochdale office in Dale Street, and passage was paid for in the sum of thirty shillings (£1.50). Two of their men appeared carrying between them the largest sill rake I have ever seen. It was of enormous length, threatening serious mischief to windows in the vicinity as they manoeuvred it about. We set off down the wide locks through the heart of Manchester. What a fascinating experience, for despite knowing the city I became lost at times, not sure exactly as to where we were. The canal weired directly over the gates instead of around the side and some of these I noted were not much better than those on the Ashton. Our two lock keepers were a friendly pair who maintained a ready chat about the canal and other matters as we carried on steadily through the locks with no particular trouble, for there seemed to be little vandalism worth the mention in this area. As we passed tall office buildings, people came to the windows to stare and wonder at a boat on the water.

Through the short Deansgate Tunnel and so to the final lock which would lower us down to the Bridgewater level, there to rejoin the canal system in better use. First we had to negotiate the lock itself which presented two problems, one being that the chamber was absolutely full of floating timber from a nearby yard, and the other that the bottom gates were chained together just above water level by the Bridgewater Department, presumably to stop all this lumber from drifting out into their waterway. We hauled some of it out to make room for NIPPY, then notified them that a boat sought a rare passage through off the Rochdale and they promptly despatched a small craft to remove the chain.

We had a little time in hand which gave an opportunity to go for a drink with the Rochdale men in order to celebrate and also mark the day. We told them our story, and when it came to the second round it was they who did the buying, for they felt that we had earned it. So back to the boat, and now we were at liberty to sail, saying farewell to the two lock keepers. "Good luck and have a good trip," they shouted as we set off, "and watch out for the barges."

I gazed behind us as we sailed away, and the future then for the canals we had gone through looked as bleak as the leaden sky above, for it seemed to me that not enough people cared whether navigation was retained, not even those with a committed interest in the canals. They preferred to sail through green fields and pastures rather than the city canals. With these thoughts in mind we turned to face the Bridgewater and to watch out for the barges as we had been told.

Cruising in the Sixties

Part One - To Llangollen

The Manchester end of the Bridgewater Canal had been deepened in order that craft of around eighty tons capacity could reach Kellogg's works in Barton, coming up the Hulme Locks Branch which connected with the Irwell and the Ship Canal. The deepening of a waterway also reduces the wash caused by a passing craft, and so it was that NIPPY slipped along at a fair speed with only a minimum of disturbance in her wake. Trafford Power Station was situated right on the bank with a whole flotilla of craft, mostly waiting to be unloaded. Of course there was other traffic. We saw another power station at Barton using water transport, and also there was a pair of Dean Waddington's narrow boats returning empty from Runcorn to pick up another load of coal from Boothstown. Young children were in the butty hatches with a long line trailing astern which I supposed to be a lifeline in case one fell overboard. I remember seeing one of the British Waterways Northern carrying fleet travelling empty towards Manchester; this short boat named BACUP looked very smart.

Our trip ended in Patricroft where a temporary mooring had been found for us in Rigbys Arm, not far from the main road bridge. We later moved to the headquarters of the Worsley Cruising Club where we were made welcome. One Doug Bennet, a well-known enthusiast on the Bridgewater at that time, had arranged all this. Duggie had recently launched a rather splendid motor cruiser of around thirty-three feet, which he had designed and built himself. EILEEN was of riveted steel construction and a tribute to her builder who made everyone most welcome aboard. The man himself was a living testimony to the lie that all Scots are mean, for he came from that country and was proud of it. His life had been a fascinating one for he had been involved in shipping from an early age and could speak with authority about paddle steamers on the Clyde. He went off to sea, serving aboard the sailing coasters which brought the china clay from Cornwall to Runcorn, where the narrow boats took over before sailing to Ireland, Dublin perhaps or Waterford, and then back to Cornwall. His adventures were many. He told of one trip where they set off for Ireland and had got two thirds of the way across when the wind dropped and the tide took them back to the English coast. Later the wind rose again and once more filled their sails and they set off with purpose for the Irish shore, only for the breeze to drop for a second time and again they drifted back in a calm sea. Finally, they had a wind continuous and fair whereby they were able to make Ireland, only to land there ravenously hungry for the owners had only put enough food aboard for the one trip and they had in fact done several. When looking for another berth he and his mates would stroll along the dockside examining the ships, especially their rigging, and if there were many splices to be seen they would usually pass on by and call her 'parish rigged'. Despite serving for some time under canvas, Duggie was by no means a keen devotee of sail. "The best rig for beating to windward is a six cylinder diesel," he would say. I came to know Duggie well, and we sometimes sailed on the canals together for he later moved to Marple. He had a mischievous sense of humour. One day we were travelling along when the horse-drawn hostel boat PAMELA came into view. "Look out boys," he said, "there's a hay burner coming!"

We had decided to stop on the Bridgewater because of the bi-centenary celebrations at Worsley where craft had already gathered in order to take part. We arrived too late to put our name down for the rally and sail past, yet attended all the same. Drifting along looking for a place to tie up, we had passed a British Waterways inspection boat when I heard a voice exclaim, "Look there it is, that's NIPPY!" We turned to look back and several heads were swiftly withdrawn. We tied up not far away in order to pay our respects but they were very wary indeed. We were guests aboard Duggie's boat for the great sail past the civic dignitaries on the steps of the old Court House. The local carriers were present with their craft all spick and span to compete for a prize. It was a day to be marked and remembered. I have been to boat rallies before and since, yet never felt an atmosphere so deep and profound as on this occasion.

The story of how it all came about has been often told before, and I shall tell it again on the grounds that a good story is well worth repeating. The Bridgewater Canal is named after its original owner Francis Egerton, third Duke of Bridgewater. The family seat was at Ashridge in Hertfordshire and Francis was the second youngest of eight children from his father's second marriage.

Unfortunately, the deadly scourge of consumption was rife among them and Francis, at an early age became the last surviving male heir. His first years had been spent not far from the Thames, where he would have developed an interest in water transport whilst watching the barges go by. Now they were determined to improve his education. The fashion then was for younger members of the aristocracy to be sent on a grand tour of Europe in order to complete their education as it were. A tutor, Richard Wood, accompanied him and amongst their visits to the great cities they saw the canals that had been built many years earlier, and in comparison to which England lagged so miserably behind. But the very fact that he inspected these waterways proves how an early interest in water transport had not been lost on the young Duke.

Returning to England, he became involved in London society and there he met Elizabeth, one of the Irish Gunning sisters, renowned for their beauty and the toast of the town at that particular time. She had been married but widowed early, and now accepted a proposal of marriage from the besotted young Francis. She thought again however and turned him down only to become the Duchess of Argyll.

Many would have shrugged this off as being one of the bitter setbacks inevitable in life. Not so the Duke. He never married, shunning London society and turning instead to improving the estates of his inheritance, most notably the one at Worsley, which was rich in its measure of coal. A big problem lay in transporting the coal to the growing market of Manchester, for English roads at that time were diabolical and almost impassable at times by wagon. They could take the coal to the navigable River Irwell at Barton where 'the Old Navigators' as they were known wanted extravagant terms for carriage to the city, and so the Duke became determined to build a canal crossing the Irwell by a navigable aqueduct, the first of its kind in the country. The St Helens Canal had in fact been built a few years earlier although nothing else happened after its completion and it never became part of the waterways network.

An urgent need for the improvement of communications had been growing over the years and the building of the Bridgewater proved to be the trigger that started the whole thing off. Many hundreds of miles had been constructed by the end of the century, with more yet to come – and all because the lady changed her mind.

Whilst on the Bridgewater, we seized the opportunity to visit the Leeds & Liverpool Canal along the Leigh Branch to Wigan, which was also in daily commercial use, most certainly with coal to the Westwood power station, where the main line was joined.

On the Llangollen

Lift bridge at Wrenbury on the Llangollen Canal

Typical bridge on the Trent & Mersey

Commercial and pleasure craft at Braunston, Grand Union Canal

Thomas Clayton's UMEA and ORWELL on the Southern Oxford Canal, 1962

Decorated boat on the Southern Oxford Canal, 1962

Diamond shaped lock on the Southern Oxford Canal

Horse-drawn dayboat on the BCN Main Line with Galton Bridge in the background, 1964

Back on the Bridgewater, we crossed over the Barton swing aqueduct several times, that remarkable piece of engineering built to replace the original aqueduct of which traces can still be seen. Naturally, the aqueduct or 'Barton Tank' as it is locally known, is swung whilst still full of water, otherwise the time taken to empty and refill would be quite out of reason, and all bridge staff were told not to leave any boats on it whilst the swinging took place. Yet their resolve for the upholding of company rules turned out to have "the breaking strain of a Kit Kat" when tempted with several bottles of brown ale, they would allow a boat or boats to stay on, affording a magnificent view of some seagoing giant in close proximity, with tugs attending at bow and stern – or so we were told.

Every boatowner we knew had been to Llangollen, so a visit there had been long overdue if only to see the famous Pontcysyllte Aqueduct. Therefore the late August found us travelling to Preston Brook in order to join the nationalised system once again. The main line of the Bridgewater turned right here towards Runcorn where a flight of locks took it down to the Ship Canal and a system of docks that at one time were very busy. The locks were later closed and filled in, most shamefully with little opposition, which certainly would not happen today.

We delved into the depths of Preston Brook Tunnel, 1239 yards in length, which at one time had a steam tug to save boat crews from the arduous and lengthy process of legging the craft through. I like this western end of the Trent & Mersey. The canal follows a wavering course as it wends its way around, at one point to pass up one side of a wood only to return down the other. It seems to be saying 'you are here to enjoy the view, not merely to travel from A to B'. Even the tunnels have caught this atmosphere, which is slightly unreal, for although they are short it is not possible to see directly through either Saltersford or Barnton since they follow a tortuous course. These were the first navigable tunnels to be built and the skill required to adopt a straight line was yet to be perfected.

I remember well the Anderton Boat Lift, which is situated not far away. We could not moor in its immediate vicinity for there were working craft gathered around, all empty and waiting for orders to load. Coasters belonging to ICI manoeuvred far below, and as evening settled in so the factories to which they came were ablaze with light.

The next day saw us passing through Middlewich, sharing the locks with another craft. A fair number of retired boaters lived here, to gather and ruminate and to watch the boats go by. Every craft would be carefully scrutinized so that if some pleasure boater made a mistake he would soon be told the error of his ways. British Waterways had a hire cruiser yard there at the time with their fleet made up partly of former working boats cut in half with a sturdy cabin added on. There also were some smaller craft belonging to the 'Water Baby' class of around nineteen feet.

We were back on familiar territory now all the way to Hurleston Junction where the Llangollen Canal begins. We passed the flight of four locks easily enough in our little boat, which was not always the case with larger craft such as converted narrow boats, for these could jam in one of the chambers that was slightly curved. The Llangollen had been legally abandoned by its former railway owners but the fate suffered by many other waterways was not imposed here. Maintenance of a kind still continued even after it was nationalised in 1948, apparently due to its supply of water from the Dee to Hurleston Reservoir, and the locks were still kept in working order. The Huddersfield Narrow was not so lucky, for it had been abandoned and navigation was not maintained although it too supplied water.

Soon we were climbing the easy locks until coming to Grindley Brook and finally the triple staircase itself. We were following two craft; a converted narrow boat named DON and one of the British Waterway's 'Water Baby' class as previously mentioned. Of timber construction, the hull was of very thick ply, which it needed to be, for this craft had been let out to somebody that I can only describe as a complete moron. He was a thickset man with two children and we saw that in going up the locks ahead of us he seemed to be doing things wrong, and a mild word of advice produced only a hard stare plus an offensive rebuke, so we all kept our distance and left him to it. Regrettably our choice of mooring sometimes coincided with his and on these occasions he would stretch his lines right across the towpath. One night a passer-by failed to notice these and tripped over, falling headlong.

The owner of DON was determined to reach Llangollen but made heavy weather of it above Grindley Brook due to the shallowness of the cut. We trailed along behind him for quite a distance until he came to a deeper part and he cheerily waved us past. I do not remember seeing him again.

Nobody could deny the beauty of this waterway on which we now travelled. There is one part where Whixall Moss is crossed, running perfectly straight through a wild peat bog with the mountains of Wales to be seen in the distance, a promise of things to come. Then on to Ellesmere, a country town situated near to the lake district of Shropshire. There is also a canal depot here, where many a sturdy lock gate has been made with an unmistakable design.

The aqueduct at Chirk reminded me somewhat of that at Marple, both having a railway viaduct alongside, and Marple once had a tunnel beyond, which Chirk still has. This was of course only a preparation for the main event still to come, and sailing onwards to pass through two locks at New Marton we eventually saw it through the trees to our right, the mighty Pontcysyllte Aqueduct. An iron trough stood on incredibly high piers, hollow in their upper part in order to reduce weight. It seemed to stretch endlessly over the valley of the Dee, reduced to the proportions of a stream far below. We realised in crossing over that reports of this being a somewhat frightening experience were certainly not exaggerated, for to one side we were now gazing straight down a sheer drop of 126 feet, which revealed once again the determination of the engineers and contractors to build a canal in such difficult terrain.

A junction to the left brought us to the final stretch before Llangollen. Where the canal beforehand was attractive and pleasant, the journey now took on a dramatic air as we clung alongside a steep hill whilst the channel narrowed until it was only wide enough for one boat, with passing places necessary even then for the increasing pleasure traffic. The canal staff clearly needed to be on their mettle in this area, for the aqueducts would soon ice over in wintertime, needing to be broken every day in really severe weather if serious trough damage was to be avoided. In addition, the hillsides we were now passing would deposit a large quantity of rainwater in the canal at times, since there is nowhere else for it to go, and a rapid rise in level would need careful water control.

A canalman walked before us as we neared Llangollen, raising a lift bridge to save us the trouble of stopping. These bridges are a triumph of the carpenter's art with their beautiful design. A horizontal frame is supported on stanchions upon which it pivots and there is a box at the inner end of this frame in order to contain the ballast. The outer end has chains which lift the drawbridge up. Boaters should note that the clearance under these drawbridges is somewhat restricted and that it is not a good idea to lie sunbathing on the cabin top whilst a lift bridge is being negotiated. Lying on top of a moving canal boat is not a good idea in any case, unless one is aware that no low bridges or low overhanging trees are in the vicinity.

And so we passed through this scenic area to arrive in Llangollen, high on the hillside overlooking the town. Perhaps eight or so craft were already there, but we found space to moor without any trouble. We liked Llangollen. The Dee flows under a bridge in the town, keeping its eternal appointment with the sea. It was good to find a restaurant and to have a meal that had not been cooked by ourselves. A day or so later we explored further up the canal using our dinghy, since we had been warned that it shallowed further upstream towards Llantisilio where there is an intake from the river.

We decided not to stay very long as a visit to Chester was planned, so accordingly one early morning found us turning her round with the idea of traversing the narrow section before anyone else got up. It is easy to see why the canal is so popular and we did it again some years later in a hire cruiser after NIPPY had been sold. Once again, it was a very pleasant trip, though we noticed that a minority of boatowners tended to be rather offhand with hire craft, merely because it is such. They should remember that in some cases visitors from overseas have hired the craft and that it can leave a very bad impression. In different circumstances they themselves would show that natural courtesy towards the visitor, which everyone expects when touring another country.

A farm situated around Wrenbury sold produce to passing craft, this belonged to the Hardern family who later operated the motor narrow boats DORSET and CHILTERN from Nantwich for camping purposes. They later moved to Beeston where their hire cruiser business was founded, so well established now.

Once Hurleston was reached, we turned left to follow the Chester Canal as it used to be, carrying straight on at Barbridge until coming to the staircase at Bunbury where the wide locks begin. Most of the craft using this canal are narrow beam so that it is possible to pass in the chambers here. The ruins of Beeston Castle stood on a promontory to our left, unmissable in the distance as we journeyed down the ancient locks to the more ancient city of Chester. No better way could be found to enter a city such as this, with its Roman wall and other antiquities combining to give a sense of history all around. We tied above Northgate Staircase to tour the city or rather a part since to see everything would have taken far more than the time we had available.

So it was that we turned her round to head back for Marple, to receive a marvellous welcome from the boatowners there who had all heard about our exploits on the Ashton, for it was a story told and told again in the bar of the British Legion Club.

Part Two - To Oxford

Our earlier journeys had taken us along two arms of the cross on which the English waterways were based. Firstly to the River Trent to test our boat on its flowing waters, and secondly to the River Severn, quiescent when we saw it yet capable no doubt of an equally powerful flow. There was yet another arm which we had only partly explored, longest of all, a finger of water extending from the Trent & Mersey at Fradley to distant Oxford on the Thames. We had to go there.

The moorings in Marple Pool had almost been empty of craft when first we had gone. Now the banks were lined with pleasure craft widely differing in design for the days of narrow boats built for pleasure had not become firmly established yet.

When travelling along the Macclesfield Canal we always tried to arrange to spend a night by Bridge 88 in Kent Green whether on the outward trip or the return. A pub called the 'Bird in Hand' stood at this quiet spot. A couple, Emmie and Jack if I remember well, kept the pub. It was really just a house with one room altered to form a bar, though the 'bar' itself was very primitive indeed without any beer pumps. The beer was brought up from the cellar in tall enamelled jugs. A building beyond had once been stabling and there was a foundry just over the narrow lane, which petered out at the swing bridge, leading only to a smallholding where an elderly man kept a few farm animals. It was a place which busy progress had missed. A time capsule within itself, yet due to the gradual increase in pleasure boat traffic its fame had reached far and wide all the way from the Grand Union to the Leeds & Liverpool.

The canal in Stoke was quieter now where once it had been the main artery of trade. The clear-headed vision of Wedgwood and others had served the potteries well, and we ourselves felt privileged to have seen the tail end of it. Even now a little trade survived. There was a pottery works called Dolbeys, bounded on one side by the River Trent, which was no more than a large stream at this point. A group of narrow boats were gathered here, some empty and others awaiting their turn to unload on both sides of the canal. We looked doubtfully at the gap between the boats, and sure enough NIPPY became wedged. It was a case of them hauling a boat away in order to free us.

Onwards we went, wasting no time for there were many miles to go totalling 175 between Marple and our goal, the enticing city of Oxford. Eventually we were on the Northern Oxford Canal, and we found ourselves waiting our turn at Hillmorton Flight of three near Rugby. These are duplicate or twinned locks side by side and reminded us of the Cheshire Locks on the Trent & Mersey. We watched as a motor boat went into one and its loaded butty in the other, hauled there by heavy booted women, advancing slowly along the lockside until finally the bottom gates were closed and they could let go of the towline. Earlier enthusiasts had speculated that boaters came from gipsy stock, for it was a view held also by the generation of their day. The boaters' roving life set them apart from others who knew little about canals even though they carried so much trade.

This ignorance extended to the men who maintained the waterways, or so I was told. Years later I worked with an elderly dredger captain who kept his occupation a secret from his neighbours because he felt that they would look down on him if they knew. All of this was of course nothing more or less than that tribal instinct which has bedevilled mankind from the very beginning, even amongst the higher echelons of thought. It is something that hopefully my own generation has put right where canal folk are concerned, for we now explore the waterways and no longer look down upon those who earn their living on the cut. In later years, I worked as a joiner on council housing estates, and the people I met on a daily basis were very similar to the boaters both in the way they spoke and in their demeanour. One watched them working as I have described, the weathered faces and old fashioned toil, the dark cabin entrance and lustre of brass – and said as one enthusiast did, "we are now in another age."

We followed them as they swung the heavy laden yet graceful craft around one bend after another until Braunston was reached and our journey took us to the right whilst they carried straight on, heading for some factory on the Grand Union which now more rarely used the canal.

We were still on the Oxford as we headed towards Napton Junction, three and a half miles away. In the thirties, a great effort had been made to increase the tonnage travelling by water between London and Birmingham, and hence this part of the canal had seen some improvement. The locks had been widened, the banks were better protected and a great fleet was built, and they did indeed succeed in competing with rail, the main rival for long distance traffic in those days. The trouble was that not enough crews could be found even during the thirties when so many were unemployed.

We came to the bottom lock of Napton Flight, which I was interested to note had bottom gates made of cast iron. We climbed our way steadily to the top and were now on the summit level. From here to Claydon Top Lock is only some four and a half miles in a direct line yet this summit pond wends its way to such an extent that it is no less than eleven miles in length. This would be an advantage in drought conditions since it would drop more slowly. Rainwater would also percolate into the canal from neighbouring fields and higher ground during very wet conditions to help boost the level.

The standard of maintenance was low compared to the northern end, with the basic requirements of dredging, bank protection, hedge cutting and so on barely attempted. As a result of this we had thought that all commercial traffic had ceased, until rounding a turn we suddenly found a pair of

Thomas Clayton tar boats bearing down on us. There was no alternative but to make for the bank as UMEA and ORWELL went past. I later discovered that they travelled between Leamington Gasworks and a tar distillery in Banbury on a regular basis.

Eventually we reached Claydon to begin the process of locking down which would take us to the level of the Thames, some thirty-four miles away. Like the Llangollen, this waterway also had quite a number of lift bridges but there the similarity ended, for these were much more basic in design. Two heavy beams were fitted to the drawbridge near its pivot point, raking at an angle with a brace going into the drawbridge outer end. A chain hung from the top of a beam and it was simply a case of hauling lustily on this until the beam was horizontal, with a tendency to close again if not carefully watched.

We passed through Cropredy and beyond until Banbury came into view with its boatyard made so famous due to the book 'Narrow Boat' by LTC Rolt. His boat CRESSY was fitted out here mostly by himself, including a bath which must have been rare aboard a boat at that time. His cruise took place during the momentous year of 1939, and so uniquely captured both the essence of travel by canal and of England as it was then, a classic which many enthusiasts have read.

Below Banbury the canal continued on its gradual descent, blending into the valley of the River Cherwell, which crossed at one point. There was a most unusual diamond-shaped shallow lock followed by a deep one at Somerton of normal construction apart from the single bottom gate.

Bottom gates on most canals are double leaf with a mitred joint by which the frames are placed in compression when the lock is filled. This way is also more economical in the use of water since the chamber otherwise needs to be longer or the single gate would foul a narrow boat when it was swung. Further on we joined the river for a mile or so, to rejoin the canal at Weir Lock, which also was of diamond shape. We then came to a wide sweep of water at Thrupp, tying overnight near a most beautifully painted narrow boat the GERTRUDE.

Oxford was not far away as we started on our final leg, to tie in that city around midday. It was, of course all that we had expected and the best way to approach it was definitely by water as with Chester in the previous year. The main thing that I remember is the impressive architecture and through it all the gentle ribbon of the Thames flowing in soft tranquillity.

Our return trip was to be varied by a visit to Coventry in order to view the cathedral recently completed there. Thus it was that a few days later, instead of pirouetting around the sharp turn at

Hawkesbury we instead turned left to sail past FRIENDSHIP belonging to the well known Joe and Rose Skinner. I met Joe later when he came north. He was retired but had been a number one or self-employed boater working on the Oxford Canal, using a mule to draw the boat.

We saw the cathedral in Coventry with its columns terminating in a pin and seeming to float just above the ground, also the figures of Saint Michael slaying the devil on the wall outside. I sympathise with the modern architect for he clearly likes to establish a style of his own yet the best proportions for a building have been thought of long ago. Not that I condemn all modern design. The interior of Liverpool Metropolitan Cathedral is breathtaking with its wonderful use of stained glass, and the circular design with an alter placed in the centre is both innovative and striking.

After a good walk around, we selected a restaurant and listened to Helen Shapiro who was often in the charts then, although she had stiff opposition because Beatlemania was sweeping the country. Their music simply reflected the times, outgoing and confident, and with very little unemployment around young people had money in their hands to spend on records, clothes and even cars. Many took their holidays abroad by this time and we were a little unusual in not travelling overseas. In the political world, General De Gaulle was still firmly saying "Non!" to the idea of Britain joining the Common Market, to the annoyance of some politicians in Westminster, who said that we should do better by joining Europe. Many were perplexed by this for we seemed to be doing well on our own.

Leaving aside such considerations and returning to our tale, we turned the boat around in Coventry Basin to continue the journey homeward by the way we had come, for to vary the route through Birmingham would have involved heavy lockage and we were running short of time. I think that it was somewhere around Tamworth where we slowly approached a road bridge, looking for a filling station as promised in the guidebook. It was a wet and rainy Sunday afternoon and some fishermen were gathered under the bridge. They had clearly sampled more than a taste of beer and there was considerable merriment. We drifted to a halt. "Taxi!" shouted the biggest of their party, a rotund man of about eighteen stone or more. He stepped heavily into our little fibreglass dinghy, which promptly dumped him into the cut and a tidal wave came through the aft windows to saturate us all. We had to go to his rescue since he was floating bottom-up in the bridgehole and took some getting out. One of his party gave us a hand but the rest were falling about laughing at what had happened. We quietly left them to it and looked for petrol elsewhere.

That autumn we entered the boat handling competition held annually by the North Cheshire Cruising Club, winning the navigator's trophy on our first attempt. The Guest of Honour would present the award at the annual dinner and dance to be held in the imposing surroundings of the Alma Lodge near Stockport. The guest turned out to be a high official with British Waterways, no less than the one who had threatened us with legal action over using the Ashton!

Part Three - To Stratford-on-Avon

The following year saw us touring Southern Ireland instead of travelling on the boat, so it was not until 1964 that NIPPY ventured far from the moorings again to accomplish her final long distance trip, this time to Stratford-on-Avon.

A journey to this famous town would not have been possible were it not for the determination of the Midlands enthusiasts, as the Southern Stratford has been badly neglected by its former owners, the Great Western Railway, to render it impassable except by canoe. It began from a junction with the Northern Stratford in Lapworth, passing through Lowsonford and Wilmcote, some fourteen miles and thirty five locks to the ornate Bancroft Basin in Stratford, before locking down into the Upper Avon, which was also unnavigable at that time apart from a short reach through the town.

The present owners were British Transport Waterways who inevitably wanted to declare it abandoned, as did Warwickshire County Council. They lost their case and it was leased to the National Trust with David Hutchings of the IWA being appointed canal manager. The idea had been to use mainly voluntary labour in tackling considerable restoration work. The army also lent a hand but despite this the project gradually fell behind. I remember spending a week there, which is saying little, since some of the Midlands enthusiasts gave much of their spare time to the project. The severe winter of 1962-63 delayed progress even more until finally in desperation prison labour was brought in, and there was light at the end of the tunnel at last. Her Majesty the Queen Mother happened to be patron of the National Trust, and so it came about that she would be re-opening the waterway in July. We could not possibly miss an event such as this.

Our journey firstly took us through territory now as familiar as an old friend, until reaching a junction with the Birmingham Canal Navigations at Aldersely on the Staffs & Worcs, commencing with a flight of twenty-one locks. These were quite easy to operate, lifting us up to Wolverhampton and the main line of the BCN, centre of the narrow canal system with canals radiating outwards like the spokes of a wheel to connect with the great rivers of England.

This remarkable complex would have been thronged with traffic only a few years before, long distance narrow boats with their graceful lines mixing with the more rudimentary dayboats carrying local trade. How interesting it must have been then. Power stations would receive their coal by canal, powerful tugs towing loaded craft, perhaps five or more blending with singles towed by a horse. There would also be transhipment points between canal and rail, so that a waterside factory could receive and consign from and to every part of the country without troubling the local roads.

Our politicians speak glibly of creating an integrated transport system, especially when an election looms, yet all that we see is a road system increasingly choked with traffic, motorways carrying far more than was intended, and where a single accident can cause a traffic jam many miles in length. What an incredible waste of time and fuel. Where is the forward planning? Where are the plans to enlarge or extend our rivers, keeping heavy traffic on the water for as long as possible? It appears that we wait in vain.

Practically all of the traffic had now gone so that we cut a lonely furrow along the main line. A half brick was thrown over some canal side fence, to ricochet off our cabin top and plunge into the depths of the murky canal with a disconsolate plop.

A bright splash of colour heralded our arrival at Worcester Bar, where the Worcester & Birmingham canal was joined. An early dispute between the two companies had caused an actual bar of masonry to be built across the junction and cargo had to be transhipped from one boat to another. Later a stop lock was built and the bar itself now provided end-on moorings for a number of craft, brightening this quiet haven in the centre of the city. There was spacious water here, which together with its surroundings of old buildings and warehouses and the distant heavy bridge, gave the junction the same atmosphere as Fairfield. A coal-laden dayboat was being discharged by mechanical means at a wharf not far away, the fact that we had noticed it showed how rare such a sight had now become.

Onwards past Cadbury's works we sailed, until at Kings Norton we turned left to join the Northern Stratford, which soon afterwards delves into a tunnel. The canal had become busy with pleasure craft, converging towards the rally. We took our turn in descending the Lapworth Locks until finally coming to the Southern Stratford, where rumours abounded concerning a shortage of water all the way down to Stratford. This meant that some of the larger craft were having trouble in travelling along which also delayed the smaller craft. Part of the problem lay with some of the boaters themselves. They would lift paddles when they should not have done and so worked against each other at times - a word of advice often going unheeded. A converted narrow boat was dragging itself along a very low pond and a group of pleasure boaters ran ahead to the next lock and prepared to fill it. "Wait 'till he gets there first," I said, but they lifted the paddles because they said their boat was behind it and they wanted to pass. With vital inches of water drawn away, the conversion simply sat on the bottom at which point it became obvious that nobody could pass except a canoe. We all struggled onwards and the compensations were that it was pleasant countryside with the weather beautifully warm and sunny. Finally Stratford-on-Avon came into view when all difficulties came to an end. A lock of barge size let us into the river to find a good mooring amid convivial company close to the theatre, where some of the cast watched the arrival of the fleet dressed in their costume.

And then came the glorious day itself, to which the sun gave its blessing right from the start. I had intended staying with the boat, watching as the royal personage came ashore, but then I changed by mind. I collected my camera and headed off into town. A great crowd was already there; luckily I found a good vantage point on a bridge. Soon afterwards the procession of craft came into view. The Queen Mother sat in the bows of LINDA, a former working narrow boat now converted for passenger use. The royal standard flew at her bows, and I suppose that on this particular day the craft could more correctly be described as a royal barge. The Queen Mother waved and gave a smile in our direction and I was able to take a photo or two.

A great many were gathered around the river lock to witness the cutting of the tape. I hurried back towards our boat and thunderflashes gave forth a deafening sound, accompanied by waving flags from all the assembled craft. She disembarked at a specially made landing stage, exchanging smiles with my father who happened to be standing nearby, probably wondering who the stocky man in open necked shirt and braces could have been, the only one there not dressed for the occasion.

The whole event was a significant day for the inland waterways of this country and to my mind it marked a turning point in the restoration cause. Formerly the waterways had been at a low ebb due to closures and other misfortunes, their supporters seen as people struggling against reality as commercial traffic drained away. Pleasure traffic was on the increase yet still not significant enough in some minds to justify keeping an entire system open specifically for its benefit, as had been said to me by an official of British Waterways, or the British Waterways Board as they were now known. Now although we were still struggling against adversity, there seemed a detectable change. The tide had begun to turn.

We ourselves found little trouble in returning up the canal. It remained sunny and warm as we travelled the main line of the BCN. A horse drawn dayboat was met in a scene reminiscent of a bygone age near to Galton Bridge, and at Wolverhampton two laden motor boats of Thomas Clayton's were underway, with a crown painted on the engine room bulkhead of STOUR, perhaps in commemoration of the event we had just seen.

In that same year, the BBC did a series of television programmes devoted to the waterways, each superbly done with an audience of millions. The result of all this publicity was a rise in the value of ex-working craft, since there were many who rather fancied the idea of owning a narrow boat of their own in order to explore their inheritance, the inland waterways of Britain.

Victory!

Our gloomy forecast over the future of the Ashton back in 1961 luckily turned out to be somewhat inaccurate. That October a meeting took place in Manchester and it was crammed to the doors. Officials of British Waterways attended, although they were seen to leave long before the meeting was over. Laurence Scott of 'The Guardian' fame took the chair with the platform speakers being Robert Aickman, David Hutchings, Martin Grundy and Leslie Morton, all of whom outlined the case for restoring this beleaguered waterway very well indeed. Morton was a man of vast experience especially where canals were concerned and it felt good to have him on our side. He had been manager of the Grand Union Canal Carrying Company and now he held a similar post with Willow Wren. A survey conducted around the Ashton established that more then twenty firms expressed an interest in using the canal, which was a little different from the line taken by British Waterways.

A proposal fostered at this time by British Waterways and local councils, was to create weirs at the locks, with the canal in-between forming lagoons. Aickman spoke passionately as to the ludicrous aspect of this. The image depicted was of some magical south sea island paradise with limpid pools and cascades, but the truth would be very different. The meeting ended on a firm note as follows, "This meeting calls for the restoration of the Ashton Canal to good navigable order, in accordance with the law; and its full use for trade and amenity."

I personally felt most encouraged by this and wrote an article for the local newspaper who were interested in the subject, being definitely on the side of the angels. It began to look as if the days of traffic on the Ashton, whether pleasure or commerce, were not quite over after all and at last we were fighting back.

The upshot of our great meeting was that a new section of the IWA was proposed soon afterwards and we were invited to attend the founding meeting to be held at the Boars Head in Higher Poynton.

Dr David Owen became chairman, David Baxter, the secretary, whilst I was asked to be treasurer. Doug Bennet also joined the committee along with my father. An IWA official explained what our purpose would be, although he also said that we were fighting a rearguard action where the Ashton was concerned.

We were firmly told that this new section was not a splinter group in any way, which tends to show that the IWA were wary of this, for in fact another branch, the North East, had split away a few years before, led by one Bessie Bunker and had re-formed as 'The Inland Waterways Protection Society'. Nothing of the sort was in our minds and we waited with interest to see how things developed, for there was talk of legal action against British Waterways. The committee meetings continued to take place at the Boar's Head amidst an informal atmosphere and there would be the occasional full meeting for members in impressive surroundings at Manchester University arranged by our chairman.

The IWA was strongest in the Midlands and South, weakest in the North, where I feel that Aickman made a mistake. He should have made himself and his ideas better known to the Northern membership, especially to the activists within his organisation, making regular visits to ensure that his policy of 'save every mile' was fully understood by all. My own impression was that not all of the IWA officialdom agreed with this view. I felt that some were quietly prepared to let the Ashton go in return for keeping others open, such as the Llangollen.

Other dissenting opinions could be heard in the area at this time especially from a faction within the North Cheshire Cruising Club who felt that a policy of appeasement would work best with British Waterways, agreeing closure of the Ashton route in return for keeping the Macclesfield open. One of their number spelt this out very clearly to me one day as we stood by Marple Junction. "Our route to the rest of the system is always south," he said, "and we never go through these." He indicated towards Marple Locks, which by that time were becoming more ramshackle every day to the concern of local residents.

We did not share this view. British Waterways had always said that all three waterways were to be closed, not merely the Ashton, which they had already achieved and the Macclesfield would be next with a bit of luck on their side. Appeasement did not come into the matter. The section carpenter at Marple had retired, yet senior management refused to allow the vacancy to be filled, telling local supervision that a regular carpenter would not be needed anymore, with any essential work being done by staff at the repair yard in Northwich.

We ourselves noticed a further decline in maintenance on the Bosley Flight such that its closure loomed as a possibility. Other arguments put forward against any Ashton restoration were that if the IWA won a legal action, the cost of restoration would simply be saved by spending less on other waterways, also the Ashton route would never be used on account of it passing through unattractive areas.

An alternative organisation to the IWA was even suggested, to be known as The Northern Waterways Association, with views more in sympathy with what they thought were those of British Waterways. A meeting of the North Cheshire Cruising Club took place in order to see if the membership would accept this new organisation. An official of the IWA bluntly responded, "Those who are not with us are therefore against us," and no more was heard of this movement.

Meanwhile we had not been inactive on the practical front. An observer section was set up so that the condition of various waterways in the Manchester area could be recorded with an emphasis on the Ashton. There continued to be occasional passages made by small craft, which could be portaged around any unworkable locks, these being the majority as further deterioration set in. Claims were also made for their being 'the last boat through' which were never taken seriously since I had been informed that they were legally out of time apart from any other consideration. The observer section also travelled the length of the Ashton around this time, using NIPPY's dinghy, although we never claimed to be the last boat through. I can still remember us exploring the mysterious little Islington Arm of Ancoats where nowadays the local British Waterways yard is established.

The winter of 1962-63 turned out to be one of the coldest that I have even known and as frost tightened its icy grip, working boats everywhere were frozen in, some of them miles from any habitation. The Grand Union coal traffic, which had been hanging on so tenuously was brought to a halt, the factories turned to road transport instead and much of the traffic was lost forever.

Of course the North did not escape this extremely cold weather. We heard that Marple Aqueduct had partially collapsed due to freezing conditions and some of it now lay on the river bank far below. How could so mighty a structure possibly be damaged by frost? There were two theories, the first being that the maintenance staff had not broken the ice which naturally had formed in the trough. This had exerted a great pressure as conditions became more extreme resulting in the stonework giving way. However, the observer for the Peak Forest had an alternative opinion. He had noticed water cascading down from one of the arches for some weeks prior to the frost. The aqueduct trough was constructed in brick with a layer of clay around it, all contained within the stone structure of the aqueduct itself. He pointed out that this water would have washed away some of the clay leaving a void, this would have filled with water and the expansion into ice inevitably did the rest. I agreed with this second theory since if the collapse had simply been caused by ice expansion in the trough, then surely the trough brickwork would also have been pushed over. Whichever theory one accepts they both share a common factor in that the local supervision had been negligent in their job.

The ice in Marple Pool was unbelievably thick. To combat this we cut a groove around NIPPY then sprinkled some industrial salt, giving more to old Bill the caretaker who went up every day to do the same until she was floating in her own block of ice, free of any pressure. The boat next to ours had a considerable inward curvature to the hull so that as the pressure increased she was gradually squeezed upwards several inches like some great orange pip which saved her from damage. Another boatowner was not so lucky, he had been chipping and levering the ice away from his craft with a pick when a chunk of it came free unfortunately taking a piece of his boat with it. We all rallied round to help whilst he fitted a temporary patch.

Naturally the feed down Marple Flight had to be turned off following the catastrophic event. British Waterways struggled for a while to maintain the level on the Lower Peak Forest by supplying it with water from the Huddersfield Narrow via the Ashton, but is was a losing battle and so as winter relaxed its icy grip, a large ugly pipe was laid, all the way from the byewash of lock number one to the far side of the aqueduct. The cost of this would have been far better spent in helping towards the cost of restoring the structure, which represented a danger to the public as it was.

The entire route continued to deteriorate with surprising speed. Bev Portman owned a hire cruiser fleet, which he operated from Timperley on the Bridgewater. He also had a narrow boat with which he had arranged to transport a load of timber for a building site on Minshull Street, near the top of the Rochdale Nine. Some of the bottom gates had become badly fouled with bricks and other items, one lock in particular being very badly affected, so he arranged for another to go ahead in order to clear the way. This was the motor boat PARROT, owned by Peter Froud, a well-known enthusiast. The IWA was also asked for their practical help and we willingly agreed. The Rochdale Canal Company had specified that the ponds could not be emptied in order to facilitate clearance work, therefore it was all the more surprising to discover that some had mysteriously been drained when we turned up in order the clear the gates over a rather wet weekend.

The project was a success and this encouraged us to try other things. I suggested that a working visit to the Stratford Canal restoration project would be instructive to us all and so it came about. We were put to work on the Wilmcote Flight, blending our efforts in with other volunteers and the prisoners already there. It was a strange experience really as I watched in fascination a doctor of philosophy and a jailed bricklayer combined in the building of a wall. The prisoners worked harder than anyone, being out in the fresh air and doing a worthwhile job instead of being incarcerated in some claustrophobic jail, which must have done them good.

The year of 1963 was very significant in that it saw the winding up of the British Transport Commission, which also meant that British Transport Waterways also came to an end. Its brief history had begun in 1955 when BTW took over from the Docks and Inland Waterways Executive, set up when most of the waterways were nationalised following the Transport Act of 1947.

The great majority of enthusiasts were against BTW and so with the passage of years it is interesting to speculate whether such antagonism was justified. They continued to operate their carrying fleet throughout the period, on both the wide and the narrow waterways, and in the latter case this meant that usually they would become the major carriers as one by one the long established private concerns gave up the struggle. A number of new craft were built during this same period, departing from the traditional style with varying degrees of success. Trade therefore existed for a few extra years, giving the ever increasing pleasure craft fraternity a fascinating glimpse of what life on the canals had really been about.

On the debit side, they caused a great deal of irreparable damage to the system, by pulling down many canal side structures no longer considered to be necessary. So it came about that toll offices, lock keepers and lengthsmans cottages, workshops and even warehouses disappeared with frightening speed. One could travel past some building clearly connected to the canal with its simple, functional lines, a delight to observe. Then soon afterwards it would be gone. Enquiries about the possible purchase of a property would often be met with a flat refusal to sell. Pleasure boaters of today feel that they are viewing the waterways as they used to be, when in fact they are boating in a desert. In addition, there appeared to be no effort made to preserve canal records for posterity. A former clerk at the Gorton Depot told me that a great deal of paperwork was simply thrown away when the depot closed, their attitude being quite simple to understand. They were only interested in transport as their title implied, not with anything else. The dying away of trade on a particular waterway also meant that the waterway had died in their simplistic view. The historical or amenity aspects meant little or nothing to them. Maintaining such a waterway was simply a nuisance, drawing funds from the larger river navigations in which they were mainly interested. So it has to be said that the winding up of BTW was a cause for celebration as far as the enthusiasts were concerned. Unfortunately, one or two of those who had applied this policy with zeal still remained when really they should have gone with it.

As time went by we continued to hold our regular meetings for the membership in Manchester with a succession of very able speakers, one of these being J F Pownall, who proposed the building of a ship canal on the 300 foot contour where there is a natural line for such a canal in many parts of the country. Of course our main aim continued to be the restoration of the Ashton route, which we discussed at our committee meetings at Poynton amid convivial surroundings in the Boar's Head. The trouble was that we were making very little progress with taking British Waterways to court and I felt that the momentum built up in 1961 was gradually being eroded, coming away from each committee with the dispirited feeling that we were going to lose.

Then came the breakthrough. An illustrated talk was given to the Marple Civic Society by one Cyril Boucher PhD, MSc, AMI Struct E, ARIBA. Dr Boucher was the Hon Consulting Engineer for the IWA. He also lived in Marple, quite close to the flight. It was he who saved the day and to whom main credit should be given for restoring the Ashton route. As a result of this meeting another was held to inaugurate the Peak Forest Canal Society. This organisation tended to be based in Marple, for it was the local residents who had voiced concern over the continuing unsightliness of the locks, now receiving little or no maintenance, and they felt that something ought to be done.

The Inland Waterways Protection Society were also involved with the PFCS at its inception, so the original committee consisted of IWA and IWPS members in roughly equal numbers, with local residents 'sitting on the fence' between the two. The early meetings could only be described as being acrimonious for there was no love lost between the two sides. Chief protagonist of the IWPS was Bessie Bunker. Descriptions sometimes give the impression that she was just a gentle old pussycat, given to writing long gossipy letters. As Bessie herself would have been the first to point out, nothing could be further from the truth. She could indeed be charming to anyone that she approved of or wished to influence. Adversaries only saw the tougher side of her nature, and that included the IWA. Sometimes when listening to her I wondered as to whom she regarded as being the enemy, us or British Waterways.

It was about this time that the Rochdale Canal Company sought powers to abandon their last remaining navigable part connecting the Ashton and Bridgewater canals by promoting a bill, somewhat unusually through the House of Lords. The success of such a bill would of course render any attempt on our part to restore the Ashton and Lower Peak Forest to be null and void. Common sense luckily came to our aid in which the Rochdale agreed to stay their hand until a final decision was made over the Ashton route.

Much heartened by this we made an application to British Waterways, saying we wished to commence voluntary work on the Marple Flight without delay. They refused but it was not a complete refusal, for we could start on the Lower Peak Forest at whatever spot we liked. We chose Romiley since the local council were on our side, offering storage for tools and equipment at their nearby depot. I well remember those early days. We would perhaps be cutting long, overhanging branches, dragging them away to be burnt or cut into logs for subsequent sale. Afterwards we would retire to a local café, tired and cold for it was wintertime when we began. The café was kept by a gentleman of Polish descent, who gave us a concoction of his own; purple in colour it certainly warmed us up!

I was surprised to receive a letter asking me to join a small committee of the PFCS, the purpose being to decide upon whether our main efforts should be concentrated on restoring the Ashton route or the derelict Bugsworth Basins, or Buxworth which the locals prefer. Our purpose was to campaign and work towards the restoration of the mainline. Nobody had ever said anything about restoring the Buxworth Basins, for this was very much a side issue at the time. I decided to have a close look before attending the meeting in order to discover what the local feeling was, and also to see first hand what state they were in.

Commencing at a junction with the Whaley Bridge Branch at Bridgemont, the canal first crosses over the Goyt and was still in water until the stop plank narrows were reached. From there onwards the channel was dry and much overgrown at that time. Then came the basins impressive in size, and where as at similar locations elsewhere there would be a sense of great activity in the past. A tramway, built in 1796, once extended to the quarries at Doveholes, some six and a half miles away. Tipplers would empty the stone into waiting craft, from where it could be boated to Marple, Manchester and many other destinations. The last limestone was loaded in 1928. Most certainly the complex had great historical value but would restoration be easy or difficult, and why was it drained off?

Seeking the answers to these questions I became involved in conversation with some of the local residents who lived in a stone built terrace overlooking the canal. One man was quite specific. He told me that there had been considerable leakage into the cellar of his house. An engineer was summoned who felt sure that it came not out of the canal but from high ground on the other side, travelling under the canal bed to emerge in his cellar. Nobody believed this, so they carried out an experiment in which a bucket of whitewash was tipped into the cut and in no time it showed in the cellar. This experiment was repeated for the engineer's benefit and it explained why the complex had been drained. I later spoke to a canalman whose father had worked on the canal before him. "They were allus very careful what they did up there," he told me. None of the residents I spoke to wanted the canal or basins restored, whereas they did at Marple.

The meeting duly took place at the home of our chairman, the excellent Howard Langley, and the question was put whether to restore the Ashton route or Buxworth Basins. There was a long silence. "Well, the main line comes first," I said, stating the obvious. A brief discussion followed and we were all in agreement, if anyone held a different view it was never expressed. We would attempt to restore the main line first, since our practical efforts at restoration had only just begun. The Buxworth Basins would be held in abeyance, to be attempted only if restoration of the mainline became an impossibility.

Not long afterwards, I attended a full committee meeting where we were given some stunning news. Bessie Bunker had requested to see the plan drawn up to restore the basins and then presented it to British Waterways as being from her own society. Of course this meant the end of any further IWPS involvement and none of their members came to the meeting. The PFCS were very upset about this and I felt annoyed at what Bessie had done. At least future committee meetings would be less fraught, with the Marple faction tending to side with us. Bessie later wrote to me, saying that I should send regular reports about the Ashton to her society. An answer was sent by return saying that I was my own man and would report to whom I liked. I also said that she was taking on more than she realised over the basins, engineering help would be needed and we fell out after that.

My opinion proved to be correct. Time and again they would carry out repairs, fill the canal only to find it leaking like a sieve and the stop planks would have to be put in again. She would insist upon using clay instead of trying other materials on the grounds of tradition. The original canal engineers used clay because it was all they had to hand. If modern methods had been available to them when dealing with a difficult section, they would most certainly have been used. Bessie Bunker was a strong-willed person, with a great knowledge of many subjects, including the inland waterways. As Doug Bennet once said, "Lucky for us she is in favour of canals and not against them, or they would all be shut by now!"

I had been scouring the canal system looking for a narrow boat for sale. I eventually found a suitable craft; she was of the deep-sided type, made entirely of steel by Yarwoods of Northwich in 1936 for the Grand Union Canal Carrying Company. Her name was LANCING. A great deal of restoration work was required and this distracted me from voluntary work on the Peak Forest. I felt that this did not matter too much since more volunteers were now available. I remember a newspaper reporter and photographer turning up on the day we had started restoration. "Huh, this lot won't achieve anything," the reporter was heard to say, which shows just how wrong people can be. Dr Boucher very sensibly moved the work to Marple Locks in defiance of British Waterways, who chose to turn a blind eye as new balance beams were fitted and repair work carried out on the gates. Some of the balance beams in fact came from the now redundant flight at Waterhouses on the Hollinwood Branch.

As time went on this restoration work gathered momentum until it spread to the Ashton itself. The Waterways Recovery Group would nominate a weekend, the ponds were emptied and hundreds of volunteers from all parts of the country would literally get in and clear the lock chambers and canal bed by hand, with debris being taken away using plant loaned by contractors or belonging to the WRG.

The Transport Act of 1968 brought an end to any lingering idea of legally compelling British Waterways to restore the route, but the campaign gradually made headway and in 1971 a decision was made in favour of restoration with money coming from local councils. A deal was also made with a large firm on the Ashton over the supply of industrial water following re-opening.

The doubters were proved to be wrong. Money was not taken from the Macclesfield etc in order to pay for restoration. British Waterways provided a new dredger to work on the Lower Peak, which afterwards remained on the Marple Section. New staff were taken on in order to do the restoration work, good working men some of whom are still with British Waterways. The unsightly parts around Dukinfield and Hyde were landscaped and now the traveller sees only mile after mile of trees as he glides gently along. Inner city life has taken over the Rochdale, whilst trouble has occurred on parts of the Ashton with louts sometimes stealing from passing craft, the towpath being a haven for drug addicts and dealers. Hopefully the siting of the Commonwealth Games close to its banks in 2002 will change all that, since the towpath is to be made into a more open thoroughfare.

The lesson has been learned. Canals do not really change all that much from one place to another. It is the area through which they pass which experiences the change. We are now seeing a most refreshing era where the waterways are concerned, with restoration schemes on every hand and a new navigation being built not far from where I live.

My involvement in the voluntary restoration campaign had been limited in comparison to others, but then I committed what many of my friends and associates in the movement considered to be an unforgivable crime. I joined the enemy!

With British Waterways

Many hours had been lavished upon my new acquisition. The rusty surfaces had been scoured clean and painted. The once vacant engine room now had an occupant, nestling between shiny new chequer plates of aluminium. Doug Bennet had done a superb job in decorating the cabin sides, so that LANCING looked in the trim as she rode to her moorings ready for use once more.

The trouble was that no work could be found. I had toured the waterways making enquiries, but the great days of carrying on the narrow canals were over and nobody wanted to know. My sole idea in buying such a boat was not to cruise around for pleasure, she had been built for commercial use and I felt determined to find something.

I worked for a long established builders in Manchester as a bench hand joiner, which was interesting enough and we were always very busy as many firms were at that time during the sixties. But it was not for me, not at that time. The workshop had no windows and needed artificial light all the while. The seasons would slip by one after the other in their measured course, yet we never saw any of it, toiling away under the foreman's watchful eye. Dissatisfaction had been building in me for some time, until on a sudden impulse I decided to make a move. Putting on my hat and coat I departed to the foreman's great surprise, taking a train to Marple.

Once there I made my way to British Waterway's Yard, knocking at the rather ornate office door freshly painted in blue. The section inspector was discussing some paperwork with the local length foreman when I entered to give them my proposal.

They only had one motor boat on the section which tended to be inadequate. My suggestion was for them to hire LANCING and myself when materials for maintenance work needed to be moved around, as I already knew a steady demand existed. The inspector turned the matter over most carefully. "You're right," he admitted, "we could do with two motor boats instead of one, because that breaks down sometimes. I don't have the authority to hire your boat, although we are looking for a labourer. Why not start for us and we could come to an arrangement for using it?

I hesitated for a moment's thought. Being a contractor was one thing, an employee quite another. It would feel most strange to work for British Waterways after all that had gone before. An enthusiast would have felt uncomfortable being employed by the old style British Waterways, yet now there was a detectable change for the better and in any case it was time to bury the hatchet. So I accepted, saying nothing about any previous activities since in any case I no longer belonged to any canal committee.

So it came about that I started for them in October 1967. The landrover driver took me down to Ashton Brothers Mill on the Lower Peak Forest at Hyde, where a couple of maintenance craft were moored with one Charlie Sherrat in charge. Charlie himself came to the cabin doorway as I stepped aboard the piling flat LORD NELSON. "Good morning young man," he said with a beaming smile, and I knew right away that we were going to get along. The cabin chimney was already smoking bravely away, they were only waiting for me. Charlie went to the other craft, a weedcutter, which today would be acting as a tug for LORD NELSON. The engine sprang into life and soon after we were off towards a bridgehole about half a mile away, badly obstructed as so many were around Hyde at that time.

Charlie rolled his own tobacco and did one for me, no mean offering this but a fat cigarette and he smoked a powerful weed. He would have been about a year off retiring then from the industry where his lifetime had been spent, for his father used to be the Marple lock keeper and they lived in a cottage at the bottom lock. He had been a dredger captain, mostly in charge of the steam dredger JOSEPH with which he had roamed all over the three waterways. In later years, they had given him a hydraulic dredger of the type we know today. He had also driven the track-laying excavators, which I was most intrigued to discover were actually known collectively as 'Navvies' to canalmen. The term is of course very ancient and I had thought it died out years ago, yet here it was still in common use to describe the mechanical successors to those teams of men opening up the river navigations so long in the past. His knowledge of the local canals was encyclopaedic as British Waterways knew. Their maps and plans of the system were by no means entirely accurate. Sometimes an official from the estates or legal departments would enquire where, for example the lines of a boundary lay. Unhurried in conversation, giving the matter a great deal of thought before answering, he was the epitome of everything I expected a canalman to be. Probably the majority would be the same as him although in this I was mistaken for he proved to be an exception rather than the rule.

I had spent a couple of days with Charlie when our landrover driver came shambling along the bank with a message that I must report to the section office in the morning. I went to the office all bright and early to see what they had in store. The length foreman collected some keys off the desk. "Come with me," he said. We went out to the wharf where an old josher motor boat lay, thoroughbred of the canals, basking in the early morning sun. She was loaded with 300 steel piles. "Deliver that lot to the piling gang at Disley and fetch her back," he said, handing me the keys. I glanced at the name on her cabin side. It was PRESIDENT.

The carriers Fellows Morton and Clayton were famous above all others for their fine fleet of steamers, of which they already had several when the firm was created by a merger in 1889. All were built with imposing names such as SULTAN, EMPEROR, KING, BARONESS – and PRESIDENT which had been launched in 1908. They were intended to work primarily between London and Braunston on what was then known as the Grand Junction, towing a butty through the wide locks. The locks from there onwards to Birmingham were narrow at that time so the cargo would be transhipped to a horse drawn craft and the tow swapped for a butty heading south with the steamer loaded again. They had an all male crew which were expected to travel 'fly' meaning to travel through the night. As diesel came into its own they were all converted to this newer type of machinery with a great saving both in space and in the numbers of crew required. Fellows Morton tended to carry lighter and more perishable cargoes such as groceries and this is why they have finer lines since capacity was of less importance.

I unlocked the doors and then started her engine, an air-cooled two cylinder Armstrong Siddely, and whilst it warmed up I lit the stove, which turned out to be a primitive affair shaped like a bottle. With everything being ready for the off I untied the lines and coiled them neatly, then shoved her out before going to the controls. Forward gear was then engaged together with some revs though not too much since a tricky bend lay ahead with pleasure craft moored on the offside. A little knot of employees just happened to be standing by, curious to see if 'the new lad' would make a hash of it. They drifted away disappointed.

I set off up the Peak on a crisp autumn morning, following the Goyt valley with its fine views opening to the left. Countryside lay all around, the trees with their leaves turned to an autumnal gold. Dark water flowed towards the stern where the propeller turned it briefly into frothy white.

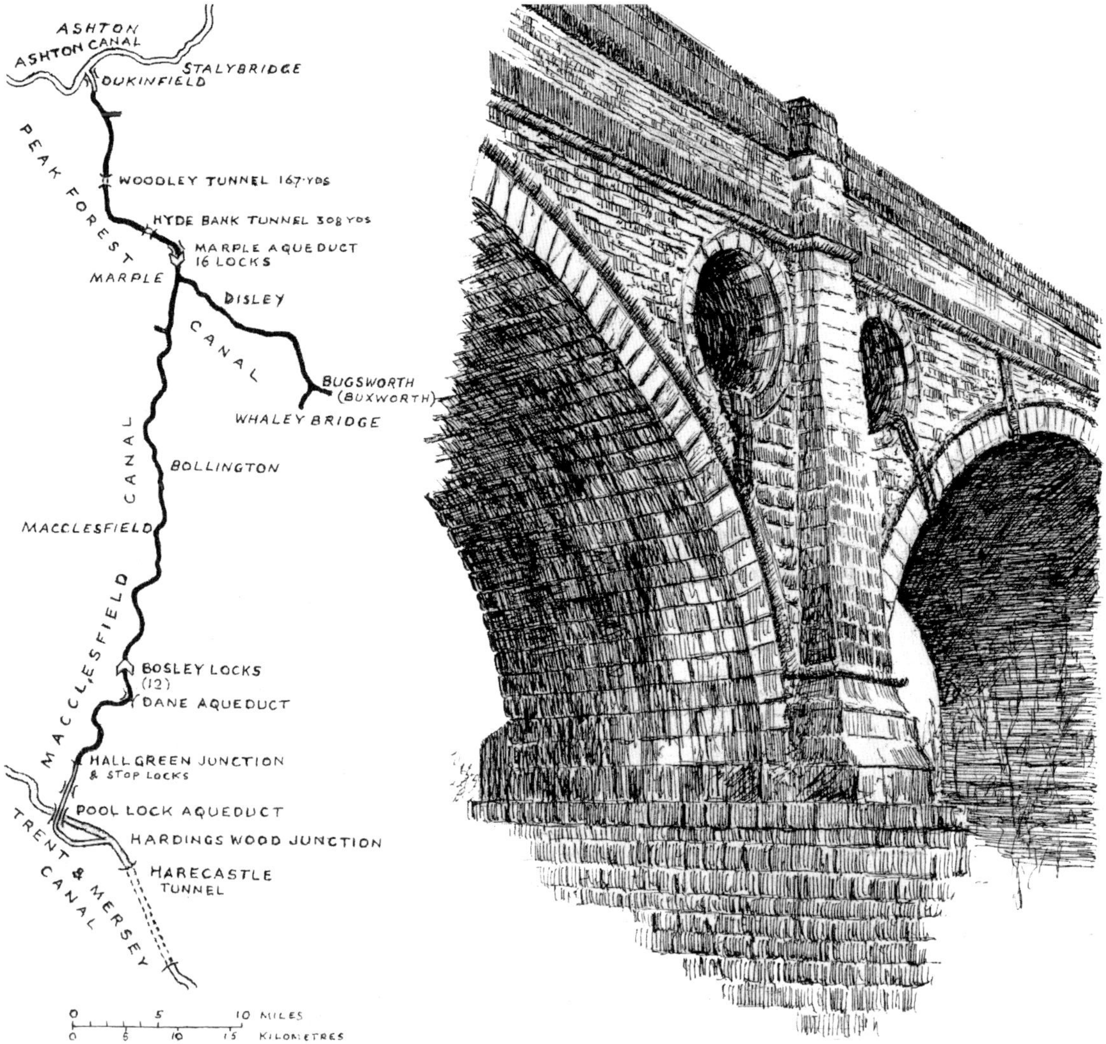

The Peak Forest and Macclesfield Canals with illustration showing the Marple Aqueduct (illustrated by Edward Paget-Tomlinson)

Only a week before I had been toiling away, enclosed in a dusty workshop and now it felt like another life, being a component of the passing scene as we went serenely along, the latest of a long line of steerers at the helm of this historic craft.

There were three swingbridges between Marple and Disley none of which presented a problem. In reaching one I would stop her with her bows on the offside bank. After swinging the bridge I took her slowly through, putting a line round the handrail post then back to PRESIDENT'S counter before taking and holding a round turn. Once she was safely out of harm's way I allowed the line to tauten such that the bridge swung swiftly back so that the round turn could be taken off and the line gathered in from its standing end without interrupting our forward progress. I once travelled on another craft and the steerer tried to do this. He tightened his line much too soon, trapping me between cabin side and bridge to sustain a badly injured foot. It is really not worth trying if there are a number of crew of board, and the practice is probably banned by now.

All too soon my destination came into view, not only seen but also heard as a raucous clatter echoed down the peaceful water indicating a piling gang at work beyond Dryhurst Bridge. We commenced to unload without delay, first putting down a couple of planks to the bank with a line of piles on top down which the others could be slid. These early piles were merely painted with bitumastic, which seemed barely adequate and proved to be the case - they are all galvanised now.

With PRESIDENT standing empty, I had a quick brew with the piling gang before setting off again to the next place where she could be turned. This was the 'Clayhole', sited in a wood between Disley and New Mills. There were deposits of clay nearby which the canalmen had been digging out for some years until forced to stop by British Railways, fearful of their line being undermined. The winding hole had been recently dredged enabling PRESIDENT to turn quite easily.

Charlie had a theory regarding winding holes. He felt that some had been created when the canal builders had come across a deposit of clay and decided to dig it out. The demand for clay must have been prodigious during the canal building age and it would explain why some are sited in rather odd places.

I made my way steadily back towards Marple. None of this seemed like work at all, so I continued long after finishing time and anyway the foreman had said to bring her back. Consequently it was early evening as we slid alongside the maintenance wharf and the engine could be stilled. I took the keys to the foreman's house. "Where have you left it?" he enquired. "I haven't left it anywhere, it's back here," I said. He looked astonished. "Took a load out and brought back the empty boat all in a day," he said. "Its never been done before!" He told me to hang onto the keys since there were more to be taken, although they could not arrange men to load until Thursday. "Clean your boat out tomorrow," he advised. He was right about the need to clean her out since she was indeed rather grubby, and the next day I stripped everything moveable out of the cabin and engine room before setting about cleaning it. Working forard, I dug the clay and chippings, remains of earlier loads, out of the hold to prepare for the next consignment of piles, before finally washing her down.

Two men turned up on the following morning. One was a labourer like myself and in speaking it turned out that he had once worked on the Llangollen. The other was the ganger for Marple length, a Spaniard whom the men knew as Tony, although it was not his real name. Tony was a hard case and no mistake, which was not surprising on account of the life he had led. He had been forced to leave his native land during the civil war - never to return. He joined the French Foreign Legion and could describe life out in the desert, as well as Paris, where they went on leave. All of this I discovered by degrees since he was not a man who would take to close questioning and the others warned me that he had a quick temper. However, there was another side to him, which showed when a child went missing in New Mills where he lived. Tony joined the police and other volunteers in searching for the little waif. He loved his adopted country, "best place in world," he would say and he meant it.

We started our task of loading the boat with piles, some of which were not directly on the canal side and had to be carried. We wore heavy gloves to protect us against the sharp edges and the still tacky coating of bitumastic paint. A simple wharfside crane had once stood here, and in fact parts of it were still scattered around like some giant child's discarded Meccano set. We often had to stride over the jib in our task of loading the piles. Later on I had an opportunity to ask supervision about this and they said it had been taken down because of the expense involved in insurance and maintenance. This meant that every time a lorry load of piles or walings came, a mobile crane had to be hired in order to unload. Also the men had to haul cement mixers and compressors up makeshift ramps off their boat, or load piles slowly and laboriously by hand, as we were now doing.

In the meantime, another more serious problem opened up for me personally. Somehow or other they had discovered my past involvement with the IWA, even though I had been careful not to say anything and they still did not realise the full extent of it. According to the Marple Length Foreman the information had been relayed further up the line that an activist had been started by mistake. The instruction received had been brief. "Get rid of him!" Luckily the high official who had first threatened legal action over the Ashton, then found himself presenting a prize for navigation, had now retired or otherwise I could have been not merely fired but throttled for good measure. "So, you have decided to leave the angels and join the rotten swines?" said the foreman. I answered carefully that the latter might not turn out to be so bad. "Well, if you want to stay here you must decide which side you are on. There will be things said and done which you will not like, but say nothing, or make no mistake you will be out." The choice was not difficult to make since even my brief time of employment with them had revealed how much there was to learn about the business of running a canal, and that I was receiving valuable practical experience. I felt like an outsider watching their daily lives and how they did things, knowing even then that one day I should write a book since so little is known about the maintenance of canals affecting all who use them.

Loading completed, we delivered it to another piling gang and afterwards were put to sailing up and down to clear the channel of any floating objects such as the banks of floating sedge, or surges as they were called, torn loose by passing craft. Some of these were really massive such that a foreman had made a tool to deal with them. He did a saw cut down a shaft then took an old scythe blade and secured it in, calling the resulting tool a dynasaw with a twinkle in his eye, and it worked. Marple Section was subdivided into two lengths, Marple and Macclesfield with PRESIDENT shared between. She was now required in the Macclesfield area which had their own crew so they took over. Tony and I were put to cutting hedges in Poynton where a work boat was already stationed.

This turned out to be the former iceboat WHALEY BRIDGE, now turned into a bank boat with a cabin added on. She had been built in the railway workshops at Gorton many years before, most robustly constructed in riveted iron with the plates finely shaped. She was barely twenty feet long, which had presented a problem during her icebreaking days, for the 'track' she left going round a sharp bend was not wide enough for the longer trading craft to follow no matter how hard she was rocked. And there were other problems. One bitter winter's day they were coming down the Peak, approaching Marple Junction and shattering the ice, rocking her as hard as they dared with a team of horses hauling mightily at the tow. They scrambled up the gradient of the bridge approach, hooves fighting for a grip and as the angle of the lines increased, disaster struck a blow. WHALEY BRIDGE came completely out to skid crazily across the thick ice, her crew thrown out with serious injury, as I understand.

The hedge had not been cut for a long time indeed and now it had achieved the stature of small trees. Out came the tools of the trade which in this case were known as brushing bills or billhooks, a kind of very heavy knife blade on the end of a nicely shaped shaft around three feet long. Sharpening stones were provided and we honed the implements to a razor sharp edge before commencing. Tony loved hedge cutting. The keen blade whistled through the air in a dangerous arc as he attacked it from all angles and I soon learned to work a distance away. We burnt the resulting brushwood on a corrugated iron sheet, dragging it along as the work progressed. We had only been two days at this when urgent orders came through to report to the yard.

An emergency had arisen. One of the craft involved in pile-driving operations at Bridgemont had developed a serious leak and had to be replaced by another from the yard. The replacement was VENICE, a josher butty boat that the section carpenter had been refurbishing. The local supervision had decided to gather us together in order to bowhaul the six miles to Bridgemont, although why they could not have asked to borrow LANCING for this I cannot imagine. A gang of us boarded VENICE in order to carry out this task. "Lade her out first boys afore we go," someone said and a large quantity of rainwater was bailed overside in order to lighten her before we set off. A good deal of bowhauling still took place on our section at that time, which the men thoroughly hated, and after plodding along hauling on a line, I came to share their view. It was not only a degrading occupation, but it was also very wasteful of labour. Some craft towed fairly easily. "She sails well," they would say. Whilst others would, "tow like a block of stone." Working on the cut often felt like living in some previous age, never more so than when towing a boat. I noticed that at mealtimes there was a definite pecking order observed by all the section. The most important one, usually the ganger, would sit opposite the fire with the others sitting where they could. The one considered least important would nearly always be found at the end.

We finally reached Bridgemont in the fullness of time, transferring a large quantity of piles, pile walings and equipment from the stricken craft. This turned out to be an old wooden narrow boat named TROJAN under the command of Albert Gosling, or 'Gozzer' to his mates. Albert had spent his younger days as mate to Charlie Sherrat on the dredger JOSEPH, but the two were quite dissimilar. Where Charlie was slow and careful in speech, Albert tended to be lively in everything that he said and did, despite his advancing years. British Waterways had asked him to stay on for a while after the age of 65, since a great deal of piling needed to be done and he was very good at it. He was interested in young people and had started a cycling club in Fairfield where he lived.

He was quite upset over the state of poor TROJAN. He and his mate had repeatedly tried the canalman's trick of shovelling dry ash from their cabin fire into the cut adjacent to the faulty seam. This ancient ploy would work for a while until the disturbance of their work caused her to leak yet again. The yard had decided to leave her in the canal leading to Buxworth Basins where she could settle on the bottom, safely out of the way. "Only a month to go and I've gone and sunk a boat," said Albert sadly, hanging his head. Nelson himself could not have mourned the loss of a vessel more. "She's rotten, Albert," said Charlie as we moved away, myself carrying the tiller as a souvenir.

My instructions were to stay with him in order to learn all about piling, and he was a very good instructor, lively again now that he had a new command and with his natural optimism coming through. As we worked he would yarn away about the canals where he had spent nearly all his working life, he talked all the more so after realising that I was interested. Many of the little tales recounted in this book have come from sources such as him.

In establishing a line of piles, he first of all drove a steel tube close to the bank where the piles were to start. Next came a line of stakes at intervals, each carefully sighted for the finished line had to follow these. Any large stones underwater had then to be moved away. A second tube was driven in around twelve feet from the first, and then long timbers were clamped vertically on either side. This left a slot through which the piles could go, the first being perfectly upright since it acted as a guide to the rest. The driving was done by compressed air. A compressor on board drove a jackhammer that impacted upon a heavy block of steel with locating pins on the underside known as the piling head. It was a very noisy, clangourous affair with no protection for the ears apart from cotton wool. Afterwards we would fit the pile walings which at that time were long lengths of angle iron with holes burnt through at intervals for the piling rods to fit. These went back to an anchor plate hammered into the towpath and so the bank was protected from the wash of passing craft again, and less prone to leakage. The final act would be for a dredger to come along to fill behind the piles, known as backfilling.

Winter now settled firmly in with a vengeance. The first wafer thin sheets of ice had appeared overnight as we trudged along the frosty bank. Within a few days this had clenched the canal in its powerful grip, strong enough to walk on and we were set to breaking the ice at aqueducts every day.

Yet another problem arose for the supervision around this time. Foot and mouth disease had smitten the countryside such that we could not go anywhere near farmland. Some activity had to be found well away from agriculture and so it was that I joined a gang with instructions to fill the potholes on a road alongside the Buxworth Basins. By this time Albert had retired. No cosy boat cabin was available now. Instead we sat shivering in a little tin hut waiting for the road stone to arrive. Heat was in theory provided by burning coal in a five-gallon drum, modified for the purpose and known as a fire devil. The smoke from this would threaten to asphyxiate us if placed too near the door. Further away we would be freezing again.

Afterwards we were moved to Toddbrook Reservoir canal feeder in order to dig part of it out as the channel was in a very silted condition. There remains a heavy backlog of work to be done on many reservoirs and feeders apart from the canals themselves. Feeders are sometimes so obstructed that only a limited flow can be delivered or it overflows the feeder bank.

A thaw set in about this time along with sorry news of PRESIDENT. She had been taken to the annual Bosley stoppage and the Macclesfield crew had left her overnight in the filled chamber of number two. The lock keeper, who should have known better, assured them that she would be safe since the bottom gates did not leak, but he was mistaken. On the following morning the lock was found to be partly emptied causing PRESIDENT'S rudder and skeg to be damaged on the sill. They took her to Northwich where she was laid up until noticed by an enthusiast of steam. I have seen her since her restoration, now famous with a steam engine installed, immaculate in black, white and red. I can still imagine Tony at the helm saying her name in his own way.

The departure of PRESIDENT meant that the section would be without a motor boat until a replacement arrived, so it came about that LANCING was pressed into service. This could not be done officially as I already knew, so arrangements were made which proved to be generous and it was on the whole a very satisfying period for me. They continued to borrow her every now and then even after the replacement arrived, which turned out to be another josher ROACH, equipped with the engine taken out of PRESIDENT.

Tony, myself and another were then put to leak-stopping on the Lower Peak Forest, where a known leak had been tending to enlarge as they usually do. The place was easily accessible by road, so we were given a van. We proceeded to load it with clay as well as a range of tools, some quite new to me. The leak could easily be seen where it emerged about half way down an embankment. In describing the size of a leak canalmen will compare volume to that issuing from a pipe. Thus it might be a one, two or three inch pipe and so on. A problem soon arose in this case. A gas main ran under the towpath and a leak could sometimes follow this for a considerable distance before emerging down the bank, so the trick lay in finding out where the clay wall had actually been pierced. Tony had been given some drain tracing dye, coloured a seemingly innocuous brown. A sprinkling of this in a jam-jar with some water added produced a most brilliant green, which he proceeded to pour into the canal at intervals close to the waterwall. We each peered intently into the water, looking to see if the dye was wisping into the stonework, an infallible sign of a leak. Luckily the surface remained calm and we were able to see. Time and time we tried, yet still it eluded us. Passers-by became curious and wondered what we were up to. Finally it was Tony who shouted in triumph. The site of the leak had been found a good twenty yards from where the dye emerged down the bank. Now we could really begin.

The towpath surface had to be dug out first, iron hard from many years of use, until the clay could be seen. Different implements were needed to deal with this material, much heavier and denser. These were known as claytools or grafters, like a spade though much more narrow, curved, and more strongly made. The clay came out easily as we worked, stacked on a clean board to avoid contamination. On reaching the leak itself we naturally plugged the gap where the water was escaping, cut out the contaminated clay and then put the clay wall back. As each piece was placed in, we pounded and pummelled it into the clay beneath, our objective being to create one homogenous mass for if the slightest crack remained, the water would make a path through again. The tool employed in doing this consisted quite simply of a piece of pitch pine, perhaps a little more than three feet in length and about three and a half inches square at the business end. Two sides were tapered from about nine inches up to make the top end one and a half inches square with a knob formed for the fingers to grip. The resulting tool was known as a punner.

Every effort was made in order to keep the work clean, making sure that no dirt remained on the soles of our boots before stepping into the trench. One thing that surprised me very much lay in the fact that no water was used at any point when putting the clay wall back, apart from lubricating the tools. Yet every canal book that I have read specifies that the clay must be kneaded with water in order to make a watertight seal. I went leak-stopping on a number of occasions and the only time that is was done in textbook style occurred when somebody from another section did indeed create clay puddle on a board, treading the water and clay together with his boots. Our lot watched him in silence before going back to their own method and I never knew their repairs to fail.

Another situation can arise when a leak has been running undetected for some time. A large cavity or void can be created under the towpath with merely a crust on top. Finally this will give way under the weight of some heavy object such as a motorbike or horse. On one occasion the front wheels of a waterway's van suddenly dropped into such a hole.

Almost every leak that I went to was sited just a few inches below surface level, enabling repairs to be easily made. My own theory regarding this is that hot summer weather can cause the clay to crack which then provides a path for the water until eventually it emerges on an embankment. The question is sometimes asked, "Does the canal bed leak?" The answer is that it certainly does but this is balanced out by water entering the canal from high ground. Another baffling type of leak can occur if the line is carried through rock and water can track through rocky fissures to emerge an incredible distance away. It is possible for water coming from higher ground to pass under the canal bed before emerging on the embankment, looking for all the world like a conventional leak. If this is suspected, the answer is to put plenty of dye in the water to see if it shows through.

Soon after this, a member of supervision was taken ill causing him to be off work for a considerable period. The usual answer in such a case was to promote an experienced man off the bank, and to my great surprise I was asked. I refused this at first, knowing that jealousy would result in certain quarters. "Refuse now and you will never be asked again," they told me.

The following Monday morning found me seated in the section office on a cold winter's day, wondering what lay ahead. The office was a throwback to former railway days when it had been the studio for an artist who painted the scenes adorning railway carriages, as older readers will recall. Another echo of railway ownership could be found in the line plans, bound in leather with the name of some long extinct railway company inlaid in faded gold. They were later badly damaged owing to water leaking through the roof.

The Peak Forest and Macclesfield totalled around 45 miles in all, with four reservoirs; Coombs (66 acres), Toddbrook (39 acres), Bosley (78 acres) and Sutton or Turks Head (15 acres), this being later taken out of service.

There was an establishment of roughly twenty men, counting supervision. These were divided into the operational workforce which included reservoir attendants and lock keepers, with the rest being classed as the engineering workforce such as tradesmen, gangers, piling gangers and labourers who later became known as canalmen. How a new starter can suddenly become a canalman on his first day was always a little beyond me. Terms of employment were different between the two groups. The engineering workforce could not be forced to turn out in an emergency outside normal working hours, although I never knew anyone to refuse. The operational men could be called out at any time, since they were usually involved with water control. The engineering workforce could not be forced to work during rainy conditions, except when attending an emergency or a stoppage.

Each man would be allocated a 'Depot', which in practice meant the nearest significant point on the canal to where he lived, and when employed in that area he would only be paid flat rate. Mostly he would be expected to travel further a field, which entitled him to 'out allowance' plus travelling time, or overtime in fact. The district was well served by rail just then, with free travel concession for canalmen to and from work. We made good use of this for one of my first tasks involved giving train passes out to men travelling from Marple Rose Hill to Higher Poynton. Another detail was that workforce could not be made to work on a section other than their own. I had tried to absorb all this and a great deal more during my first morning at their Marple office.

The duties of supervision could be briefly given as follows:

Section Inspector (or S.I.)

〈 Responsible for seeing that the section is run with economy and within budget limits, also that work delineated in the annual budget is being carried out.
〈 Expected to attend where a difficult task occurs and to make decisions.
〈 Responsible for maintaining discipline among the men and settling matters regarding pay and hours.
〈 Expected to see all his men every week and to take an interest in their welfare.
〈 In overall charge of water control.
〈 Issued with a waterway's vehicle and on a salary that increased according to years of service.

Length Foreman

〈 Directly responsible for supervising the men and seeing that they kept to time.
〈 Responsible for checking the line of canal as well as reservoirs and feeders.
〈 Seeing that any materials required were delivered on site and passing any grievance or enquiry on to the inspector.
〈 On an hourly wage plus overtime.
〈 Issued with a motorbike, classified as operational staff and a water controller.

The section was changing from motorbikes to vans at that time, so they lent me four wheels instead of two. A packet of correspondence arrived from the area office at Northwich around 9am, which we discussed over a cup of tea. Mostly it was mundane stuff, easily settled over the telephone. As the days quickly passed, I fell into the pattern and routine of running the canal, which any enthusiast would have enjoyed. After seeing what the men were up to I would get the landrover driver to take me out, Whaley Bridge perhaps or Bollington and walk back along the towpath to Marple, making note of anything needing attention as I went. The embankments were covered in a carpet of snow making leak spotting much easier since it could be seen as an ugly black line cutting through the virgin whiteness. Another responsibility was to check any vulnerable points or places where the bank was thought to be weak or if there was low freeboard.

On Thursday we had to make up the wages before paying the men. Payslips would have arrived from Watford on the previous day, complete with coinage analysis so that we only had to visit the bank in order to draw it out. This would always be following the same route carrying a briefcase, no doubt an obvious errand to any watching villains. Perhaps they considered that it was not worth the effort bearing in mind the poor wages that canalmen were being paid then.

On Friday we would code up the time sheets for posting to Watford where all the calculations regarding wages for the entire waterways network were done, every section having a code number, ours being 404. Canal and reservoir reports always went to the same area office and these included a statement as to canal levels on that day. A plus or minus level would involve doing a complicated calculation.

Weeks quickly blended into months and I continued as acting length foreman, sometimes looking after the Marple length or sometimes the Macclesfield. I came to know the local waterways and their environs very well and it turned out to be a most satisfying occupation. Not that everything always ran smoothly. One would imagine that administering a canal must be a peaceful, relaxing experience with every activity guided by generations of practice, which was simply not the case. They could fall out over the slightest thing, such that I could go into the office with an argument in full swing. The positive side of this was that afterwards literally everyone knew what the outcome was, but in fairness I should add that running a canal is by no means always a simple task.

The main one involved in these fiery debates would usually be Jack Brown, the Macclesfield length foreman. The canal always came first with him, which made us of one accord. He constantly warned his men about getting the sack but had never fired anyone in all his years as a foreman. They all knew this of course, so it was generally a case of in one ear and out the other, though he kept them on their toes. Most had been with him for years. He had his own pet name for many items, which could be a little confusing at times.

The same applied to some of the older workforce who often spoke in a manner and dialect that I did not understand at first. One was Jack Gibson, or Gibby as we all knew him. He was the reservoir attendant at Bosley and Sutton, and a great character with a long service record. One day, whilst we were seated in the Sutton hut, he suddenly said, "Theer's a rot on the bonk sithi." "A what?" said I, gazing in the same direction before seeing what he meant. It was a rat on the bank.

The drivers of a coach firm all knew Gibby and would give him a lift as he trudged homewards after a night out in Macclesfield, following the meandering country lanes with the passengers no doubt wondering why they had left the main road and were suddenly on a mystery tour instead of heading for London.

The section had no dredging unit of its own at that period, despite the appalling shallowness in places. We had to borrow the unit based at Red Bull on the Trent & Mersey every year, consisting of the dredger HAMSTER, captained by Jim Taylor, along with several mud boats, a tug and a navvy for unloading. The mud boats were a mixture of former working butty boats and purpose made mud hoppers, which the men told me were very awkward to steer. They would make their way to the Upper Peak Forest, pausing en route to do spot dredging such as at shallow bridgeholes, or digging out a mooring for some boatowner. There would also be a considerable amount of backfilling behind piles which had been driven during the previous year. These were straightforward tasks that did not require the navvy or its driver, so they would usually be sent off the section unless something else could be found, otherwise a charge would be made on the section account.

I should explain here that any boat or item of plant supplied from Northwich would be charged to the section just as though it had been supplied by a plant contractor. This even applied to craft regularly kept on the section such as the motor boat. The rule did not apply to other craft which had always belonged such as the old iceboat WHALEY BRIDGE.

Line dredging could begin in earnest once the Upper Peak had been reached. An agreement would have been made with some local farmer or landowner for dumping the spoil, ideally in some canalside valley which would help to level the land. At one time they were dredging on the Macclesfield in the lonely Pearsons Valley, bringing up many a ton of coal which had been shovelled overside during the carrying years in order to save unloading time when the destination was reached.

We could not hold onto the dredger more than the allotted period of weeks or there would have been trouble for of course the section could not do exactly as it liked. A budget would need to be prepared every year in which the most important tasks needing to be carried out would be decided. The engineers would then say how much of this could be done in order to remain within the budget. Of course it was not possible to anticipate any unforeseen problems arising within the year which could throw financial statements awry. The underlying problem lay in the fact that a considerable backlog of work existed. We were gradually reducing this on the Marple section, yet a great deal remained to be done.

A dispute had arisen some time before between Marple section and the Ashton. They believed that water coming down the Huddersfield Narrow was also feeding our Lower Peak Forest, and that we must have a considerable leak somewhere. This was firmly denied by Marple. "A leak of that size would show on the embankment," a length foreman said. Finally the Ashton men put stop planks in on the Tame Aqueduct where our two sections joined. Sure enough after a day or so it was seen to be weiring over towards Marple, but the matter had still not been resolved when the planks were taken out during the re-opening work.

My turn as acting length foreman came to an end and to my delight I was given the motor boat ROACH with its neat boatman's cabin. My mate turned out to be a quietly spoken Macclesfield man by the name of Tommy Warrington. Tommy's main hobby was backing horses and he knew every bookies for miles around and I took an interest in it for a while until realising that one could lose a great deal of money participating in this addictive sport. We were mostly taking basic materials out from the yard, or generally clearing the canal of floating stuff in between loads as spring returned again.

One bright morning in early May, we were just preparing to cast off when a message arrived from Marple. The section carpenter was finishing and the inspector would be coming out to offer the job to me. We turned the engine off again to discuss the matter over a brew. I felt happy enough on ROACH and did not fancy the idea of 'going back on the tools' as it is termed, but Tommy thought I would be a fool to refuse. "It's promotion," he said, "and they will be disappointed if you turn it down. Anyway, you won't always be working on this boat, you know how they move us around." He was right of course, especially on the latter point which decided the issue, and when the inspector arrived I was able to give him a definite answer.

So it came about that a few days later I unlocked the heavy door and entered the carpenter's shop to take full stock of the place. It was large and well lit, occupying the upper floor of what had originally been a warehouse. An arm of canal passed right through underneath with a door enclosing either end, whilst a trap door in the well-worn floor indicated where goods had once been lifted up. The maintenance yard had at one time been located at the bottom of Marple Flight with the remains of buildings still to be seen. Two great coils of hempen rope were draped on either side of the door, relics of former icebreaking days, whilst templates hung from the whitewashed walls for the yard used to make its own wooden carts and wheelbarrows. There was a tradition here firm enough to stand on and it would suit me very well. The Marple length foreman was welcoming but warned, "there's a great deal of work to be done, not today but starting tomorrow." He was wrong in the latter respect for not long afterwards a pair of feet could be heard pounding up the steps, a sound which I came to know well. It was Jack Brown. "The top gates at lock number two Bosley aren't fitting together," he said. "I want you out there right away." The driver took me to Bosley where Charlie the keeper stood anxiously waiting. "Something needs fixing," he said, "water's pouring round the gates." I went down with him and sure enough a fair torrent cascaded into the chamber. We spanned the lock head with a plank and inserted stop planks into the grooves, treading them down before inserting wedges. A lifted paddle soon emptied the head so that I could scramble down to see what was the matter. It turned out to be part of a tree root wedged below the lip of the sill and holding the gate off. I removed it with difficulty, satisfied that the trouble had been found. All of the surrounding woodwork looked dilapidated, so I measured the paddles and guiders for replacement which would provide something to do.

Back at the shop, I sorted out two pieces of elm that would be suitable. The best way of making paddles is to keep the number of pieces to a minimum, holding the device together with two paddle pins, with one end forged into a block and threaded at the other. The elm needed to be bored out accurately which in the past had been laboriously done by hand with an auger. "How long does it usually take to make one?" I asked. "Oh, about two days" was the answer. They had a heavy-duty electric drill available, so I set this up on a drill stand and made an adjustable frame below it to secure the paddle whilst it was bored out from both sides. Afterwards I heated up an old paddle pin in the fire until the end glowed an orange-red before driving it in through the holes in turn to give clearance for the pins. The outer face received its heavy rebates for the guiders then the inside or working face needed first trueing with a plane before a three inch margin could be marked all round.

Using stop planks to drain a lock head
(illustrated by Edward Paget-Tomlinson)

A paddle tends to bow slightly in use due to water pressure, which in turn makes it rub against the paddle frame during lifting and very hard to draw, therefore the centre needs to be hollowed out. There is only one tool able to do this satisfactorily and it stood on the floor awaiting sharpening and use, it was a carpenter's adze, known to woodworkers during Roman times if not before. The tool is very rarely seen nowadays, yet it still remains in use on the canals, retained not for tradition's sake but because for certain purposes it is ideal for the job.

The centre was soon hollowed out following which I placed the completed paddle, the first of many, into a well filled with water, there to be kept until required. I have described the making of a paddle mainly for the interest of those thousands who travel every year on our canals, and when applying their windlass to ground or dandy paddle gearing might wonder what is on the other end.

There will be variations but the principle is the same. Elm is the timber used because it is softer than oak and more readily takes up the inevitable wear instead of the cast iron paddle frame, and it is more easily replaced. Also it does not need treatment of any kind if left immersed in water. In the fitting of these paddles, the paddle rod had two 'L' shaped pieces at its lower end with large holes through which the pins could then be tightened down which left only the horizontal bolts through the rod, to be checked and renewed if there was much wear. These are the ones which sometimes shear when the paddle is allowed to drop freely either by a novice or by the more approximate boater, a sin guaranteed to earn a disdainful glance or even a rebuke from any nearby lock keeper.

With these paddles fitted, I returned to the yard where another much greater task lay ahead. A stack of timber had arrived for the making of stop planks that would keep me busy for some time. Twenty sets were needed with six planks per set and all needed reducing at the edges with the adze. I had my list of sizes and started straightaway in cutting the twelve by four sections to length. Every plank needed checking to ensure that any knots went on the compression side. Of course if there were too many of these the plank could not be used. Out came the adze to apply that graceful curve at either end, which is done in order to give spring to the plank like a hammer shaft, where a taper will be found close to the head. A plank to be worked would be secured to the floor and the adze swung between the feet, its weight and sharp cutting edge making it dangerous to use, and one of the few edge tools that is used towards the carpenter. One day, distracted by somebody else the corner went into my leg just above the ankle and there was blood everywhere. It is not unusual for a canal carpenter to bear the marks of an adze, although one I met a few years later, a fine man off the Bridgewater, could not show me the location of his scar because he had sat on the implement.

Following this, a heavy chamfer needed to be cut in the lower edge of each so that a ledge was thus formed with the square edge of that below so as to trap the racking when it was shovelled in. A hole needed to be bored and a pin inserted towards each end to prevent splitting. Then after the handles had been nailed on, the final operation was to burn in the relevant bridge number.

During the making of these I was largely left on my own which gave me ample time to wander around the yard seeing what they had. The warehouse-cum-garage carried a fair amount of working tackle, though it could have been better equipped. There was an implement known as a prick bar, about nine feet long and nearly an inch in diameter, sharpened at one end. Its first purpose was to be driven into the towpath in order to trace a suspected leak. Secondly, it could be used for driving into the sill behind stop planks if these were thought to be weak. A chisel shaped object on the end of a shaft was known as a spud which also came into its own in the fitting of stop planks where the grooves needed cleaning out. When preparing to fit stop planks, the men usually found something on the sill which would first need clearing off, for example stone perhaps where a sill rake was the ideal tool. Sometimes the sill would be heavily silted over and a sill rake was of little use. Here an iron scope could be employed, this being a sort of scoop at right angles to the shaft. There were also wooden scopes of a quite different design for scooping water out of a lock chamber that could not be shifted by a pump, though I rarely saw these being used. I also noticed a heavy hammer much larger than the rest, which gloried in the name of 'Enoch'. There was also a winch which came in handy at times plus an assortment of ladders and scaffolding for use in the locks.

Other little jobs cropped up, not strictly to do with carpentry, but welcome all the same for they were experience gained in looking after the cut. One emergency occurred when vandals boarded a maintenance craft only to smash their way into the cabin and they took a pick with which to pierce the steel hull. The stricken craft drifted into Hyde Bank Tunnel where she sank which had obviously been the intention. There is in fact considerable damage caused each year to our waterways by people with malicious intent. The only thing we could do was to put the stop planks in and drain a length which included the tunnel. With this done we still had to enter the tunnel in a small rowing boat provided by myself.

John, a canalman and myself set off equipped with lights, waders and buckets for bailing purposes, also I made one or two wooden plugs to hammer into any holes. The entry of this tunnel was an eerie affair not improved by our insufficient lighting and being semi-drained as it was. We came across the boat, now with gunwales above the surface, boarded her and started to bail. I expected water to come up from the holes yet none appeared as we toiled away to reduce the level inside. In fact we had her almost empty yet still she remained on the bottom. "How can this be?" I thought as I set my bucket down. Then it occurred to me that the flat bottom had created suction in the glutinous mud and that she could not rise. As I realised this, John rocked the boat and she suddenly came up with a rush. We paddled her out of the tunnel with me feeling that I had experienced enough floundering around in the darkness for a while.

Once back at the yard, I commenced repairs to the damage, although we could not find any holes that had sunk her, until one day somebody noticed what appeared to be a pit hole larger than the rest. I prodded this with my finger then found myself doing a little Dutch boy act as water spurted out all over the electrical tools. Someone brought a plug, then as I hammered it in another spurt started beside it as all the sealing mud fell away.

In dewatering the canal, a large hole in the rocky bank had been found near Marple Aqueduct. It was the inlet hole of a leak which ran for perhaps two hundred yards before exiting on the riverbank.

The process of dewatering a section could be done by using what the engineers termed let-off valves, and local canalmen knew as 'box trunks' or 'paddle trunks' depending on the type. The first as its name implied consisted of an oaken box with a hole in the top at one end. A heavy block of elm sealed this off with a rugged hinge at the towpath end and a chain at the other which simply lay on the canal bed until the trunk needed to be opened. They would search for it with a rake and either pull the lid open directly or perhaps use a roller provided on the bank. Water then went through this box via a culvert into some nearby stream or river. One drawback of this type lay in the fact that once opened it could not be satisfactorily closed again until the canal emptied, which made it useless for water control. Also a dredger could cause problems by accidentally grabbing the chain since the location of every box trunk is not always known.

Draining a section by opening a box trunk. Unsuitable for water control.
(illustrated by Edward Paget-Tomlinson)

The paddle trunk is more sophisticated and can be used for water control. I was sent out to repair a number of these and it was obvious that they had been inoperable for quite a long time.

So the year went smoothly on as summer spanned its pleasant course. As autumn turned into winter our thoughts dwelled on the stoppage to come. Two pairs of upper gates had worn off their fit against the stonework and sills and a torrent of water was running to waste. The answer was to cut grooves into all mating surfaces in order to fit liners of either rubber or oak in a process known as lining out.

With all arrangements made, I arrived at Bosley top lock on a frosty winter's morning where the two boats appointed for the stoppage had already arrived. The motor boat ROACH had towed WHALEY BRIDGE specifically for my own use and complete with carpenter's mate, one Ernie Steele, an engaging character from Macclesfield. We toiled all day getting things ready, transferring equipment to the craft before getting them into position, then turning the feed off and emptying some of the lock ponds. As we worked through the short winter's day, the sky gradually turned the colour of slate. That night a great blizzard swept over the English countryside and by morning the little lanes going down to the flight were fully blocked with snow. I fretted badly at this since it was my first stoppage and I wanted no delay. "Doan tha worry Jim," said Harry Moseley, the ganger, quite unruffled. "It allus snows at stoppage time." Conditions abated after a couple of days which enabled us to resume the stoppage once again.

Our first task was to clear the large volume of snow lying around the lock head of number four. The collar bands were eased out a little to allow for the extra thickness, then I cut out a groove along all the mating surfaces which turned out to be quite a task. The oak was quite soft to begin with, but as my chisel bit in deeply there came that toughness that one associates with this timber. More wear was found at the bottom of each gate owing to greater water pressure. We had decided to try rubber for the first pair, except for the mitres where a greater width is needed. With this pair completed, we dropped down to number five which had also been leaking badly. This time we used oak liners, which proved to be more successful because it was possible to obtain a better fit. After cutting a groove as before, it received two layers of a specialised felt, after which the liner could be secured with fasteners known as pan head nails. Final fitting could be done by first painting the stone quoins (pronounced 'coins') with a harmless dye known as red raddle. The gate was then closed so that a mark would be made indicating the parts to be planed. This marking and planing carried on until the gate was in contact all the way down. Sometimes the chippie's patience runs out before this is achieved. In fact it was possible to make a very close fit with a wooden liner, for it would eventually bed into the stonework so that even the mortar joints would be accommodated. Many top gates needed refitting, but some were too far gone with rot and needed replacing, which we eventually did. They were somewhat pernickety in the fitting therefore it was all the more satisfying to make them totally watertight. Finally we made careful note of all maintenance still outstanding before filling the ponds again. Traffic was still fairly light at that time so we were able to carry out several early morning stoppages during the following months in order to reduce the backlog a little.

It is bad canal practice to have leaky lock gates without doing something about it. Few gates are totally watertight but if the volume passing through is excessive the pond above will be drawn down. A penstock is often to be found by the topmost lock. This is opened sufficiently to allow a metered flow down the flight sufficient to keep the lock ponds at weir level. Naturally it has to be opened more if the gates are in need of repair and so vital water is lost.

Meanwhile my parents and I had moved into a waterway's cottage at the depot, standing close by the junction of the Peak Forest and Macclesfield. Built around 1820, it had once been the toll collector's cottage with a little office overlooking the topmost lock. Circumstances dictated that I should live there for a while on my own when I noticed that the place creaked quite a lot, especially at night and my thoughts inevitably turned to the supernatural. "Nonsense," somebody said, "anyway if there are any ghosts they will only be canal folk." This reassurance failed to comfort me, somehow.

Now we could almost see NIPPY at her moorings from our bedroom windows, which was marvellous. The cabinwork had been deteriorating for some time so we stripped her right down to the gunwales and built on a new cabin to a different design. My father had now retired and they would often set out on a day cruise when the weather was fine. They had bought a budgie from Jack Brown, who bred them and the bird would go on the trip as well, chattering away all the time. Back home it would help to call the cat in, from the safety of its cage.

A consequence of living so close at hand was that inevitably I would be roped into any emergency that occurred. One bitter winter's night the phone rang. It was the inspector. Somebody had reported a leak in the bank beyond Marple Aqueduct that afternoon and the message had only just come through. Would I collect our driver and have a look? I called for him and we explored the bank as requested, armed only with a little torch. No leak could be found as we advanced carefully along. A strong wind had now developed into a full winter's gale as we passed by the stand of high trees, their branches clashing together as though at war. Finally we found it. Water ran out from a masonry wall, not at one point but for quite a distance along. It was a bad leak. "What do you think?" I asked the driver. He was a surly type at the best of times, but experienced none the less. "Dunno," he said taking a step back. The leak looked really bad, but would it give way overnight or hold until morning? The problems involved in organising a workforce and either tackling the leak or putting stop planks in at that time of night loomed up before me. Suddenly in a flood of confidence I knew that it would hold, and told the inspector so on our return.

As spring gave way to summer again, so the reservoirs became more in demand. The approved practice was to draw evenly on all four as opposed to one at a time, the reasoning here being that if a breach should happen it may isolate a reservoir left full and the canal could be short of water. The possibility of a breach occurring has to be at the back of every canalman's mind, for it is a case of 'when' rather than 'if' such an event will happen and rapid action would be required.

Often I would be alone in the yard and sometimes I would hear the office telephone ring, wondering what it could be. Eventually I had a key made so that at least the phone could be answered and any message jotted down. One day, close to finishing time, I answered the phone expecting some usual enquiry, but this time the voice was urgent. I listened with growing dismay to the terse sentences, asked a question or two and then hung up. It was a breach.

I considered the situation, realising that the regular supervision was not around and that I would have to take charge. Only two men were in the yard, one of whom was a liability. I let him go then collared the other and we briefly discussed our options. We thought that stop planks would be needed since the breach sounded bad. In any case we had nothing to transport the heavy stop planks in, no transport of any kind except for my Austin A55. I scribbled a message on the office notepad then we shoved some tools into the boot of my car and made rapid progress to Padden Brook, Romiley where fortunately the situation was now less serious. The canal had indeed breached the bank. It was an overflow breach caused by subsidence of the towpath leaving a low freeboard. The canal had risen such that the running water formed a deep furrow or cleft. A house on the newly built estate had taken the brunt and part of the canal had flowed through the back door and exited through the front, with the rest merely taking a detour around the side. Sacking had been placed along the bank weighed down with planks from a local factory. I noted that the canal level had already subsided below the bank again, so there was no immediate prospect of a full-scale breach. It had in fact been a breach in the making.

The order of events in a full-scale overflow breach runs as follows. In rising well above its normal level the canal will find some vulnerable point where there is low freeboard. It runs over, cutting a cleft, which is easily done if the ground is poor. The water wall is then left unsupported and collapses at that point, leaving a clear run of water through. One might imagine that a full size breach would take many hours to form, but it is not the case, for once the embankment has been saturated it then floats away a section at a time until in extreme cases a mighty hole is formed, as demonstrated to us a few years later. Naturally there had to be an investigation into the cause, revealing that a considerable volume had entered off the Ashton causing it to overflow the bank in many places. This led to the building of a spill weir at Ashton Junction.

Another factor which saved a breach was the way in which the canal level dropped again. Why did this happen? Spill weirs can take a certain amount, although it overflows at surface water pressure, which sometimes is not enough to speedily dispose of a large volume. On this occasion a discharge from the bottom of the canal is required. This is achieved by opening one or more paddle trunks. During prolonged, heavy rainfall the level inevitably will begin to rise, how much will depend upon certain factors. A strong wind could alter the level on a long lockless length such as we had, but the main factor to be considered was the saturation level of high ground adjacent to the canal. If a wet spell had been preceded by a drought, then the ground acted rather like a sponge and the water controllers usually have little to worry about. It is a different tale if the ground is already wet.

Our section had the luxury of a rain gauge at Bosley Top Lock and the lock keeper would be consulted as to the reading before reaching a decision. The water controllers did not act independently. Instead there would be consultations over the phone and if it seemed that action should be taken the order would come, "Open up!" Certain paddle trunks would then be opened with the men ringing back to confirm that they had done so. The canal engineers would be informed whatever the time, day or night. Wisely they left decisions over water control to the local staff who knew their waterway best. Generally the system worked rather well, although like everything else in life it could be let down by human failing.

On the evening of 13th July 1973, there began a continuous torrential downpour lasting all through the weekend until late Monday morning on the 16th. Newspapers later carried stories of abnormally wet weather throughout the country showing the damage caused by floods. Early on Monday morning I glanced at the water gauge in New Lock opposite the cottage. It showed above the level, though not dangerously so. I imagined that the water controllers would be opening up so I went round to the office but it remained unlit with no vans parked outside. The workforce arrived soon afterwards and went into the canteen. We were repairing Marple Locks at that time and many extra men had been taken on, including my own little department. Later I went to the office again. There was still no sign of life. Of course, they must be out on water control I decided, and sat down with the other men for there could be no prospect of doing any work in such heavy rain.

Later that morning, I saw a water controller staring into the canal, coat over his head since it was still pouring with rain. I joined him and felt horrified at what I saw, for the level was now much higher with the gauge not even visible. We looked at each other in disbelief. Where had all this water come from? He raced towards his van, driving off in a great hurry to do more water controlling and as he went so the rain ceased to fall. I looked again at the level, far higher than I had ever seen it, and I knew in a moment that it would breach, murmuring my thoughts aloud. "Is it, do we go on water control then?" It was the carpenter's mate standing behind me. "Too late for that," I told him after a little thought. The time for water control had passed. Our canal was about to make a paddle of its own. We had to find out where.

A vulnerable point existed which we often thought likely to breach. We would go there and also check out a culvert nearby. The driver had not turned in; luckily the keys had been left in the ignition in accordance with orders, and so we threw some tools in the back before setting off in haste. The vulnerable point seemed to be holding well though I noticed water jetting straight out from a land drain on the other side which must have been happening all over the section. The culvert had begun to block with a lake starting to form, so we cleared it with a rake before returning to the yard.

All had been peaceful and quiet when we left barely an hour before, but now pandemonium reigned supreme. Men were galloping about, hauling away at the great pile of stop planks encouraged by our inspector who had appeared, armed with a tape rule and working faster then anyone else, quite opposed to his usual laid back style, which was a bad sign. "Something's happened at Disley, I think the bank's gone!" he shouted in my ear. The stop planks were shoved into the van after which we all crammed in, breathless from the effort. I fairly belted along with all lights flashing, scattering other traffic including a fire engine coming the other way. We turned down by 'The Dandy Cock' to finish on a narrow, rutted track, bouncing madly along to close the canal at an angle and slightly above it. The most appalling sight met our eyes. A high embankment was missing over a distance of perhaps twenty yards, and over this mighty chasm the water thundered like Niagara.

Our party hastened to the nearby swingbridge with all possible speed. The level here had drawn down by perhaps two feet with water rushing silently through to crash over the breach no great distance away. A single rickety plank was flung across and a young canalman ventured onto it, sill rake in hand, balancing precariously above the flow. If he had fallen in he would have been swept to his death. He felt along the sill with his rake to report the presence of just one large stone. "Leave it there and get the planks in," said our boss urgently, so we did as instructed.

The first were pinned sideways due to the rush of water so we had to use others on edge in order to force them down the grooves. With all of these inserted the great body of water was now stopped except for some still issuing out beneath the planks caused by the presence of the stone. Workmen from a nearby factory had inserted stop planks to seal the canal on the other side some time before; luckily these were kept by the bridge.

We still had this minor torrent to deal with and the question was - how? After experimenting with one or two ideas, we finally went back to the time honoured way of filling small sacks with clay, forcing them into place in order to form a reasonable seal before stepping back to the next stop plank narrows where we had time to make a better job.

The Macclesfield gang had now turned up and were set to work opening a box trunk between Disley and Strines. They fished the heavy chain out easily enough yet the lid simply refused to budge no matter how hard they tried. Finally, I lent them a set of chain blocks which solved the problem.

Later that day another weak spot turned up in which the surface of Strines Road below a canal embankment, not far from our yard, came up by about two feet and a long, deep crack could be seen in the embankment. Standing on this spot I followed with my eye the likely track of any breach between here and the distant river. I noted the many houses in between, and realised how lucky British Waterways had been as we set about inserting planks at this second location, for had the breach at Disley not occurred, I feel that the bank would have failed here. Naturally, a second set of planks had to be installed before this weakened section could be partially dewatered in order to take pressure off the embankment. These had to be inserted a distance along the Macclesfield since there were no grooves either at the Junction Bridge or Church Lane. The day was already well advanced with evening shadows beginning to form as we completed this final task of the day.

On the following morning some of the men were detailed to inspect the banks in case other damage had occurred. Information had come through that the Black Brook at Buxworth had been the culprit and a great volume of water had filled the basins before overflowing into the canal itself, with more coming through the paddle hole, which normally kept the basins drained. The inspector and I went to investigate, finding a large area of flattened grass and other signs indicating that it must have occurred even though the brook was now more quiescent, burbling away many feet below. I later heard that an obstruction in the brook course had caused the water to back up and overflow.

Afterwards, I visited the stop planks with a water controller who had been doing the length foreman's job, and we were amazed to find that the level was up again despite all the water discharged through the trunks and the incalculable quantity gone through the breach. The owner of the moorings opposite Marple Junction corroborated my evidence of a swift rise in the level. He also mentioned having seen a 'step' advancing past his moorings which had us rather baffled.

Reports came in of water having been right over the towpath further up the Peak, such that people were putting fish back into the canal as the level dropped. I firmly believe that it was only the towpath wall, or boundary wall as it is sometimes mistakenly called, which prevented a breach in a number of places.

A breach had in fact occurred at the identical spot in the early forties when both planks had been taken. A stream course runs underneath at this point where the culvert had become blocked. The deep valley had filled which caused the banks to be washed away. The canal workforce had repaired the breach without reinstating the towpath wall. A post and wire fence had been used instead, the remains of which can be seen in the fine photograph by Gordon Mills.

A picture now began to emerge. The canal ran for miles along the side of a river valley with high ground to one side of it all the way, sometimes very steep. A great volume of rain had fallen over a wide area, which first settled into then ran down the fields and hills to the only place where it could go – the canal. In addition the Black Brook normally small and nondescript, had overflowed its banks to pour thousands of tons of water into a canal never designed for the purpose so that in effect it became a river without an exit and a breach was not only likely but inevitable, for the sluicing power of the district could not possibly match this volume. The embankment at Disley had in fact settled a little, giving a lower freeboard and this, together with the absence of a towpath wall, is what caused a breach in that location.

Peace never reigned for long in the Marple Office as already stated, especially in the wake of the breach. Harsh words were said unsupported by facts, most of it driven by self-preservation.

The 'Ice Boat' WHALEY BRIDGE

An adze - ancient woodworking tool still used on the canals

Cutting groove for gate liner

Making top gate pattern, Peak Forest Canal, Marple

The Disley Breach

Everyone knew that the water controllers had not acquitted themselves well. They were not directly responsible for the breach of course, being due to freak conditions, but the proper procedure had not been followed. One controller had gone on holiday and the others had not taken this into account. They failed to make provision for the missing link until it was too late.

Naturally there had to be an enquiry by senior management, which looked carefully into the matter. Blame was then laid in a certain quarter regarding water control, with new arrangements being made all of which to my mind were correct and justified.

By this time I had arrived at some definitive conclusions regarding my employers at that time. The remarks that follow are not intended to apply to any one section or area since I also travelled the canals where the thoughts of other employees could be sought.

A great deal of criticism had been levelled against British Waterways over the years. Some of it came from those with a political axe to grind against a nationalised industry, which thereby makes it invalid. There is no such thing as a perfect organisation, irrespective as to whether it is in the public or private sector. Many industries do, it is true, function best under the beady eye of the private operator, but our waterways do not fall into this category. If public ownership is no good then it says not a lot for the emergency services, the NHS, local councils or the armed forces, on all of which we depend absolutely.

The policy at that time was to employ enough men to cover the emergencies that arose, since maintenance work in abundance could be found for them to do the rest of the time. In later years, the policy was to deplete the workforce or even to shut a depot or two, giving contractors some of the work formerly carried out by canalmen. This was a misguided policy. Ask a long service employee off the Trent & Mersey about the Grand Union and he will be vague in his answer. Ask him instead about his own local waterway and he will be a mine of information. He would also know what to do in an emergency, which cannot be the case with some 'here today gone tomorrow' contractor. The men tended to be left unsupervised for long periods of time and there were some who took full advantage of this. One answer might be to bonus target the more regular tasks such as dredging, bank piling and hedge cutting, the latter of which is nowadays done by machine.

Traditionally the posts of length foremen, inspectors and local supervision were usually filled by the tradesmen of British Waterways, which had been the practice even during railway ownership. In later years the difference in pay between tradesmen and length foremen was reduced such that many of the former no longer felt it worthwhile to seek promotion. This resulted in the posts being filled from other sources, which was not always a success especially when new work was being carried out. It does not always follow that a good tradesman will make a good supervisor, but a man who has been through the discipline of apprenticeship is more likely to make a success of supervising new engineering work for example, than one who has not.

The canal engineers were always courteous to the men, asking some question perhaps and listening carefully to the answer. Naturally, they knew far more about the engineering side than we did. We could put stop planks in at a breach but it was the engineers who schemed out what to do next. When dealing with recalcitrant supervision it seemed to me that they would sooner harangue a man to try to make him do better or move him somewhere else rather than cause him to seek other employment. I also felt that some local supervision around the system were given far too much latitude in that they were able to do very much as they liked during waterway's time.

Canal administrations carry a heavy responsibility for ensuring that their waterway is not a danger to any nearby properties, bearing in mind that a good deal of building has taken place alongside waterways as their popularity has increased. Breaches apparently are less common now, possibly due to the heavy commitment towards piling the banks. Another type of breach can happen when a culvert carrying a stream course underneath the bed collapses. Canal staff must be ready for any such emergency, inserting stop planks or opening paddle trunks as required. There must be a firm policy regarding stop planks as to whether or not they can be left on site. Vandalism is of course the trouble here and a storage box will be made on site in some areas, although this itself could be attacked. They should definitely be on site in the neighbourhood of a vulnerable point. Paddle trunks should always be kept in usable condition, for an installation that cannot be used might as well not be there.

The maintenance of these and other vital elements should not be left to the whim of some local supervisor. A better system needs to be thought out, perhaps having a canal and river inspectorate within the framework of British Waterways.

As repairs were started to the breach we could return to our main task, that of restoring the great flight of locks at Marple. They proved to be much wetter than the ones at Bosley where a two-inch pump proved to be adequate. Marple needed much heavier plant which unfortunately was not available since it had already been commandeered for restoring the Ashton and elsewhere. We were forced to use contractor's plant, although this turned out to be totally unreliable such that at one lock we tried one pump after another. Our lock keeper kept a tally and it came to twelve, one of which caught fire. The restoration began to fall behind schedule with blame falling upon the workforce. Later on we were given a four-inch Sykes Univac which speeded up the restoration considerably. We had begun at the Top Lock, being based at the yard nearby. This continued to be our base for the entire restoration period, despite the ever-increasing distance involved. Nevertheless, we all had a feeling of deep satisfaction as the first craft sailed through to attend the Ashton reopening. As somebody said, "these locks will be here long after we have gone."

The maintenance of Bosley Flight continued, with the fitting of a new pair of bottom gates. The pair to be replaced were certainly old, one opinion being about ninety years though it could not be verified through records. I have found it very difficult to say how long the timber will last. Some gates installed by myself are still in use whereas others fitted at a later date have needed to be replaced. Clearly there is a variation in the quality of the oak which I put down to the type of soil in which the tree has grown, a dense heavy ground producing a hardier tree in my opinion.

The first step was to measure the gates; this was done by a foreman and carpenter coming out from the Northwich Repair Yard. These same men also made the much larger Weaver gates, so I already knew of their expertise. A standard formula using simple geometry was used for measuring up gates and seemed to work very well. This was an attractive spot and during the dinner hour the carpenter excused himself to go for a stroll along the bank. "Every place we go he always likes to take a walk," said his foreman. I understood. I too had once been stuck in a workshop for years.

With all the dimensions carefully checked they returned to their workshops, busy in the production of new gates. Finally the message came that they were ready for delivery along with a three-leg derrick to hoist the gates into position, although I personally preferred a gantry.

In the meantime we had our own preparations to make; the way in which it would be done, the numbers of men needed with boats and equipment and finally where to dispose of the old gates. Jack Gibson turned his feed off and then as stoppage day dawned we set up the steel derrick with its apex over the centre of one gate. A spike at the base of each went into small holes prepared by the stonemason. All gearing had to be taken off together with the jackhead, and then it was the turn of the balance beams. These cantilevered members turned out to be made of oak and were mighty heavy indeed as six of us struggled with them across the lockside. Normally we would then have inserted the gate lifter into a hole bored through the top rail, but these gates were so ancient we dare not try it except to ease them into a better place for lifting. Consequently, a buckling chain had to be put around part way down for the actual lift itself. The gate was hoisted as high as it would go until a boat could be slid underneath to take each gate in turn. With these cleared away, we could float a second boat in containing the new gates, which were in turn lifted out and leant at the side of the gatewell.

Now we could drain the pond and chamber, which still left some two feet or more of water to be dealt with. Earlier I had made two 'stanks' as they were called. One was about four feet high, the other one smaller but each had rounded bottom edges to correspond more or less with the inverted bottom of the lock. After clearing away any mud, a bed of clay was laid either side of the gatewell and a little way up the wall. The stanks were dropped into these beds, the deepest one furthest into the chamber, not vertically but at an angle with their tops towards the gatewell. They were then driven hard into the clay. A heavy wedge was hammered in at each end, the principle being that the differing pressure between top and bottom of the stank would drive it more tightly into the invert.

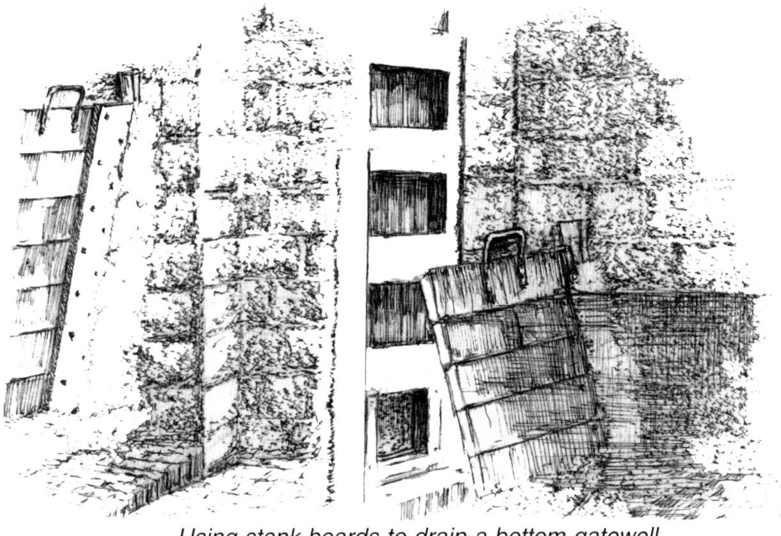

Using stank boards to drain a bottom gatewell
(illustrated by Edward Paget-Tomlinson)

Canalmen toiled away lowering clay by the bucket load and treading it into position with wadered feet until we were ready to start our pump. As the little machine clattered away, so the water in the gatewell lowered, and we sealed any fountains that still managed to pass the clay.

Finally, I could see the level floor of the gatewell and studied the sills. These were of oak and in lovely condition, needing only skimming on their mating faces to be true once more. The sill pins were screwed into lead-filled cavities in the stone, all in all a very secure arrangement. The use of lead had been abandoned a few years before on account of the safety aspect, since molten lead and dampness most decidedly do not mix. Behind me two men had spotted a lost windlass at the same time and swooped on it like a couple of gannets. The bottom of a lock gate is located by a pintle turning in a cup, not truly round, but elongated slightly in the direction of thrust. This pintle might be found in the gate heelpost or the lock floor depending on local custom since working practices can vary.

With all of this sorted out, it was time to step the first gate on with its rounded heel sliding down the hollow quoin at the top as it was lowered away. The U-shaped collar band could then be inserted through two anchor straps which are in turn fastened to the anchor stone below. With the others still hauling on the rope, I slipped the heavy washers on then hammered the gate cotters in, and they let go of the rope with sighs of relief. With both gates stepped on, I adjusted them so they were both tight into the quoins and we tried them together. They were correct at the bottom although rather too full at the top and would need trimming with an adze.

I marked them with a long straightedge as they put some scaffolding in on which I could stand. The trick was to avoid taking too much off so I carefully left the line in for final dressing or ‘kerfing down’ as it was called. In doing this, the gates were put tightly together using props and wedges in order to maintain pressure at the joint. A couple of sawcuts down the mitre would give perfect contact with the sills.

Some serious sawing was called for here and our yard possessed the very thing, a magnificent two-handed rip saw with great peg teeth, easily five feet in length. Using a ladder on each side, one leaning out and the other in, we commenced to saw down the mitre and as we worked the sawdust fell in a golden shower of tawny oak. After a while, a wedge had to be inserted at the top otherwise the pressure could bind our saw. I discovered that too much pressure at the mitre could be a bad thing since the saw then found it easier to deviate alongside its true line. We reached the bottom and then planed the cut below the sill. Once more and everything was fitting perfectly, I couldn’t even insert a knifeblade into the sill joint.